A Reading Book in Ancient Irish History

For Young Teens

BY

P. W. JOYCE

VISIT OUR IRISH-AMERICAN BLOG SPOTS

The Irish American Tribe
theirishamericantribe.blogspot.com

The International Irishman
theinternationalirishman.blogspot.co
m

The Irish American Trail
theirishamericantrail.blogspot.com

The Wee Blog of Irish Blessing and
so on
theweeblogofirishblessingandso.blog
spot.com

When Washington Was Irish
http://whenwashingtonwasirish.blog
spot.com/

The Wee Book of Irish Jokes (Book
support blog)
http://theweeblogofirishjokes.blogsp
ot.com/

The Wee Book of Irish Recipes (Book
support blog)
http://theweeblogofirishrecipes.blog
spot.com/

The International Irishman
http://theinternationalirishman.blog
spot.com/

The Wee Blog of Irish Blessing and
so on
http://theweeblogofirishblessingand
so.blogspot.com/

The Irish in their Own Words (Book
support blog)
http://theirishintheirownwords.blog
spot.com/

The Connecticut Irish (Book support
blog)
http://theconnecticutirish.blogspot.c
om/

The Irish Tuohy's of the World
http://tuohysoftheworld.blogspot.co
m/

States of America
http://theirishstatesofamerica.blogs
pot.com/

Connecticut History
http://connecticuthistory.blogspot.c
om/

A big blog of Irish Literature
http://abigblogofirishliterature.blogs
pot.com/

PREFACE.

As this little book is intended chiefly for children, the language is very simple. But to make matters still easier, all words and allusions presenting the smallest difficulty are explained either in footnotes or in the "Notes and Explanations" at the end.

Advantage has been taken of the descriptions under the several Illustrations to give a good deal of information on the customs and usages of the ancient Irish people.

Although the book has been written for children, it will be found, I hope, sufficiently interesting and instructive for the perusal of older persons.

The book, as will be seen, contains a mixture of Irish History, Biography, and Romance; and most of the pieces appear in their present form now for the first time. A knowledge of the History of the country is conveyed, partly in special Historical Sketches, partly in the Notes under the Illustrations, and partly through the Biography of important personages, who flourished at various periods from St. Brigit down to the Great Earl of Kildare. And besides this, the Stories, like those of all other ancient nations, teach History of another kind, very important in its own way.

Ancient Irish Manuscript books contain great numbers of Historical and Romantic Tales; and the specimens given here in translation will, I am confident, give the reader a very favorable impression of old Irish writings of this class.

CONTENTS.

The Voyage of Maildune.

Ornament from the Book of Kells.

I.

LEGENDS AND EARLY HISTORY.

In our Ancient books there are stories of five different races of people who made their way to Ireland in old times, with very exact accounts of their wanderings before their arrival, and of the battles they fought after landing. But these narratives cannot be depended on, for they are not real History but Legends, that is stories either wholly or partly fabulous. Of the five early races, the two last, who were called Dedannans and Milesians, were the most remarkable; and they are mixed up with most of the old Irish tales.

The Dedannans, coming from Greece, landed in Ireland; and having overcome the people they found there, became masters of the country. They had the name of being great magicians; and ancient Irish writings are full of tales of the marvelous spells of their skilled wizards. They remained in possession for about two hundred years, till the Milesians came, as will now be related.

For many generations the Milesians, before their arrival in Ireland, journeyed from one part of Europe to another, seeking for some place of settlement. And becoming at length weary of this state of unrest, they consulted their chief druid, who was a skillful seer, and bade him find out for them when they were to end their wanderings, and where they were to settle down. The druid, having thought the matter over for a while, told them that far out on the verge of the western sea was a lovely green island called Inisfail,[2] or the Island of Destiny, which was to be their final home and resting-place. So they set out once more, and fared on from land to land, keeping the Isle of Destiny ever in mind, thinking of it by day and dreaming of it by night. At last they arrived in Spain, where they lived for a time. Here they were under the command of the renowned hero "Miled of Spain,"[3] or Milesius, from whom they came to be called Milesians.

Some old Irish writers say that while they dwelt in Spain, their chiefs, as they gazed wistfully over the waters northwards, one clear winter's night, from the top of a tower at the place now called Corunna, saw Inisfail like a dim white cloud on the sea, in the far distance. However this may be, the eight sons of Milesius, after their father's death—many centuries before the Christian era—set sail with a fleet, and soon arrived on the coast of Ireland. But before they could land, the Dedannans, by their spells, raised a furious tempest, which wrecked the fleet and drowned five of the brothers with most of their crews. The remaining three landed with their men; and having defeated the Dedannans in battle, they took possession of Ireland.

A fairy hill: an earthen mound at Highwood, near Lough Arrow, in Co. Sligo.

When the Dedannans found that they were no longer able to hold the country, the legend tells us that they retired to secret dwellings under old forts, moats, cairns, and beautiful green little hills: and they became fairies, and built themselves glorious palaces in their new underground abodes, all ablaze with light, and glittering with gems and gold.

From that period forward, till the time of the Danes, there were no more invasions; and the Milesian kings and people were left to make their own laws and manage the country as they thought best, without any interference from outside.

In the History of Ireland from the settlement of the Milesian Colony down to the time of St. Patrick, that is, to the fifth century of the Christian Era, there is a mixture of legend and fact; and it is often hard to disentangle them, so as to tell which is truth and which is fable. As we advance, the truth and certainty increase, and the legend grows less, till we arrive near the time of St. Patrick. From about this period forward, we are able to tell the main history of the country without any mixture of fable.

For a long time in the beginning the Irish people were all pagans; and the kind of religion they had will be presently described.

As early as the third or fourth century—long before St. Patrick's arrival—there were some Christians in Ireland; and it is believed that the knowledge of Christianity was brought to them from Britain: but on this point there is no certainty. Their numbers gradually increased as time went on; and when St. Patrick arrived he found some small Christian congregations scattered here and there through the country. But the main body of the people were pagans; and to St. Patrick belongs the glory of converting them. The history of his life-work[Pg 5]need not be told here, as it will be found set forth in one of the Chapters of the "Child's History of Ireland." It is enough to say that he arrived in the year A.D. 432, with many companions to aid him; and that after thirty-three years of constant toil, he died in 465, leaving the great body of the people Christians, and the country covered with churches. St. Patrick was a man of strong will, of great courage—fearing no danger while doing his Master's work—and possessing mighty power over those he mixed with and addressed. He was more successful than any other missionary after the time of the Apostles.

Some years before St. Patrick's arrival, a great king ruled over Ireland (from 379 to 405) called Niall of the Nine hostages. From him were descended most of the kings who reigned over Ireland after his time till the Anglo-Norman Invasion.[4]

From the earliest ages the Irish of Ulster were in the habit of crossing the narrow sea to Alban or Scotland, which can be seen plainly from the sea-cliffs of Antrim; and many settled there and made it their home. In the year 503, nearly forty years after St. Patrick's death, a great colony of Irish—men, women, and children—crossed over, commanded by three princes, brothers, named Fergus,

Angus, and Lorne. In course of time the posterity[Pg 6]of these people mastered all Scotland; and from Fergus, who was their first king, the kings of Scotland were descended. At that time Ireland was generally known by the name of Scotia, and the Irish were called Scots; and from them Alban got the name of Scotland.

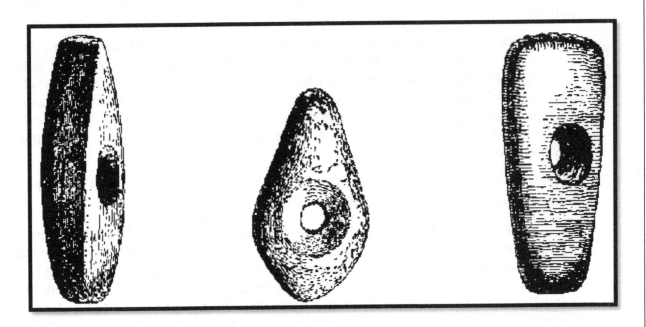

Stone Hammers, used when metal was still scarce, or not known at all. A wooden handle was fixed in the hole. Iron was known in Ireland from the beginning of the Christian era, and gold, silver, copper, and bronze, long before it.

In old times there were five provinces in Ireland:—Leinster, Ulster, Connaught, Munster, and Meath. Meath, which stretched from the Shannon eastwards to the sea, and from Kildare on the south to Armagh on the north, was about half the size of Ulster. It was the last formed of the five, and later on it disappeared as a province altogether. The present counties of Meath and Westmeath occupy only about half of it. In those times, the county Louth belonged to Ulster, and Cavan and Clare to Connaught.

There was a king over each of the five provinces, and over these again was a king of all Ireland, called the Over-king or head king. The kings of Ireland had their chief palace on the Hill of Tara in Meath; where many of the forts and other remains of the old buildings are still to be seen. But Tara was deserted as a royal residence in the sixth century, after which the kings of Ireland lived elsewhere.

II.

THE SONG OF INISFAIL.

I.

They came from a land beyond the sea, And now o'er the western main, Set sail, in their good ships, gallantly. From the sunny land of Spain. "Oh, where's the Isle we've seen in dreams, Our destined home or grave?"—Thus sung they, as by the morning's beams. They swept the Atlantic wave.

II.

And lo, where afar o'er ocean shines A sparkle of radiant green, As though in that deep lay em'rald mines, Whose light through the wave was seen.[Pg 8]"'Tis Inisfail—'tis Inisfail!" Rings o'er the echoing sea, While, bending to Heav'n, the warriors hail That home of the brave and free.

III.

Then turn'd they unto the Eastern wave, Where now their Day-God's eye A look of such sunny omen gave As lighted up sea and sky. Nor frown was seen through sky or sea, Nor tear on leaf or sod, When first on their Isle of Destiny Our great forefathers trod.

THOMAS MOORE.

III.

THE RELIGION OF THE PAGAN IRISH.

So far as we are able to judge from our old writings, the pagan Irish had no one religion common to all the people, and no settled general form of worship. They had many gods; and it would appear that every person chose whatever god he pleased for himself. Some worshipped idols; and we read of certain persons who had spring wells for gods: while some again adored fire, and others the sun and moon. The people also worshipped the *shee* or fairies, who were supposed to live in grand palaces underground, as described at page 3. The persons who taught the people all about these gods were the Druids, who were the learned men of those times. They were believed to be wizards, and some think that they were pagan priests.

The pagan Irish had a dim notion of a sort of heaven, a happy land of perpetual youth and peace. It was believed that there were many happy lands in different places, which were called by various names, such as Moy-Mell, I-Brazil, and Tirnanoge. Some were out in the Atlantic Ocean, off the western coast, while others were down deep beneath lakes, and some in caves under forts or cairns. They were all inhabited by fairies, who sometimes carried off mortals: and those whom they brought away hardly ever came back. A fairy who wished to allure a mortal often chanted a sort of magical song called an incantation, which exercised a spell over the person that listened to it.

There is a pretty story, more than a thousand years old, in the Book of the Dun Cow, which relates how Prince Connla of the Golden Hair, son of the great king Conn the Hundred-fighter, was carried off by a fairy from the western shore in a crystal boat to Moy-Mell. One day—as the story relates—while the king and Connla and many nobles were standing on the sea-shore, a boat of shining crystal approached from the west: and when it had touched the land, a fairy, like a human being, and richly dressed, came forth from it, and, addressing Connla, tried to entice him into it. No one saw this strange being save Connla alone, though all heard the conversation: and the king and the nobles marveled, and were greatly troubled. At last the fairy chanted the following words in a very sweet voice: and the moment the chant was ended, the poor young prince stepped into the crystal boat, which in a moment glided swiftly away to the west: and prince Connla was never again seen in his native land.

THE CHANT OF THE FAIRY TO CONNLA OF THE GOLDEN HAIR.

I.

A land of youth, a land of rest, A land from sorrow free; It lies far off in the golden west , On the verge of the azure sea. A swift canoe of crystal bright, That never met mortal view—We shall reach the land ere fall of night, In that strong and swift canoe:[Pg 11]We shall reach the strand Of that sunny land From druids and demons free; The land of rest, In the golden west, On the verge of the azure sea!

II.

A pleasant land of winding vales, bright streams, and verdurous plains, Where summer, all the live-long year, in changeless splendour reigns; A peaceful land of calm delight, of everlasting bloom; Old age and death we never know, no sickness, care, or gloom;

The land of youth, Of love and truth, From pain and sorrow free; The land of rest, In the golden west, On the verge of the azure sea!

III.

There are strange delights for mortal men in that island of the west; The sun comes down each evening in its lovely vales to rest:

And though far and dim On the ocean's rim It seems to mortal view, We shall reach its halls Ere the evening falls, In my strong and swift canoe; And ever more That verdant shore Our happy home shall he; The land of rest, In the golden west, On the verge of the azure sea!

IV.

It will guard thee, gentle Connla of the flowing golden hair, It will guard thee from the druids, from the demons of the air;[5]My crystal boat will guard thee, till we reach that western shore, Where thou and I in joy and love shall live for evermore:

From the druid's incantation, From his black and deadly snare, From the withering imprecation Of the demon of the air,

It will guard thee, gentle Connla of the flowing golden hair; My crystal boat will guard thee, till we reach that silver strand, Where thou shalt reign in endless joy, the king of the Fairy-land!

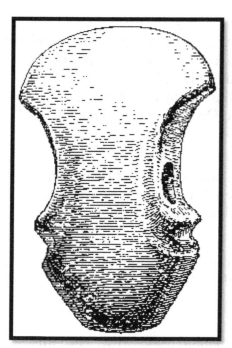

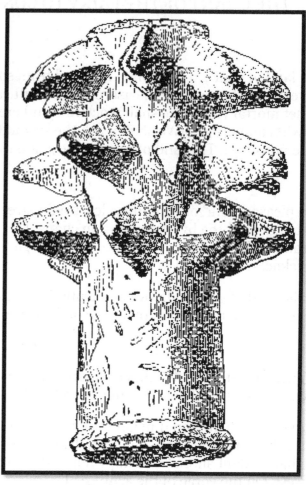

Stone hatchet in the National Museum, Dublin: probably used as a battle-axe. Before metals came into general use, tools and weapons of various kinds, in Ireland as well as in other countries, were made of stone, flint being commonly used for making cutting-instruments, such as knives. But this was at a very early period, mostly before the time when our written history begins.

Bronze head of Irish battle-mace: now in the National Museum Dublin. It was fitted with a handle which was fastened in the socket; and it was used for striking in battle. It is double the size of the picture. Weapons of this kind were in use at a very early time, long before the beginning of our regular history.

IV.

CUSTOMS AND MODES OF LIFE.

Our old books contain very full information regarding the Irish people, and how they lived, more than a thousand years ago.

In early times Ireland was almost everywhere covered with forests; and there were great and dangerous bogs and marshes, overgrown with reeds, moss, and coarse grass. Many of these bogs still remain, but they are not nearly so large or dangerous as they were then. Great tracts of country were uninhabited, so that the whole population was much less than it is now.

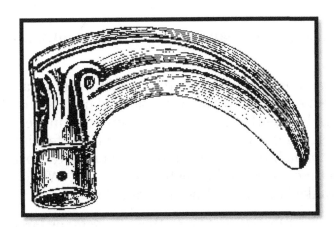

Ancient Irish bronze reaping-hook: 6 inches long. It was fitted with a handle which was fastened in the socket with a rivet. Now in the National Museum, Dublin.

The people hunted and fished a great deal, partly for food, partly to rid the country of noxious creatures, and partly for sport; for the forests were alive with wild animals of all kinds, and the rivers and lakes teemed with fish. But no one then thought it worthwhile to hunt foxes and hares for sport, as people do now. They had much grander game:—wild boars with long and dangerous tusks; gigantic deer; and fierce wolves that lurked in caves and thick woods. In the cleared parts of the country there was much pasture and tillage various kinds of corn and vegetables were grown, and the land was very fertile and well watered with springs and rivulets.

A moat: at Patrickstown, near Oldcastle, Co. Meath. Some moats were burial mounds.

There was more pasture than tillage; and the pasture land was not fenced in, but was grazed in common. The law was very particular in laying down rules about the fences of tillage lands—that they should be properly made, and that when two farms lay next each other, each man should do half the fencing work. Oxen were generally used for ploughing: horses seldom. Generally two oxen were put to one plough, but sometimes four, and sometimes even six. While one man held the plough, another walked in front to lead the animals.

On account of the great forests and bogs, there were many large districts where it was hard to go long distances across country from place to place: and often impossible. But in all the inhabited parts there were roads or cleared paths. The roads of those times were however very rough, and not nearly[Pg 16]so good as our present roads. Rivers were crossed by bridges made of rough planks or wickerwork—for there were no stone bridges—or by wading at shallow fords, or by little ferry boats.

The people lived in houses almost always made of timber, generally round-shaped or oval, but sometimes four-cornered and oblong like our present houses.

In order to keep off wild beasts and robbers, there was a high embankment of earth, with a deep trench, round every house. Many of these earthworks still remain all over Ireland, and are well known by the names *lis*, *rath*, fort, &c.; and some have high mounds commonly called moats.

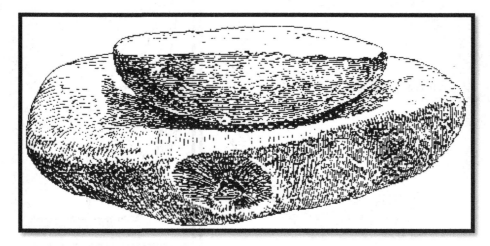

Grain-rubber: 16 inches long. People ground their corn with this before the invention of querns and milk. The grain was put between the two stones, and the upper stone was worked backwards and forwards with the hands. It was very hard and tedious work.

The food of the people was not very different from what it is at present, except that they had no potatoes, which were brought to Ireland for the first time about 300 years ago: and there was no tea or coffee. They used oats, wheat, rye, and barley, ground and made into bread; fish; and for those who could afford it, the flesh of various animals, [Pg 17]either boiled or roast. Oatmeal porridge or stirabout was in very general use, especially for children. They ground their corn with small watermills, or with handmills called querns, one of which was kept in almost every house. Querns were in use before the earliest time that our history reaches; and water-mills were introduced before the arrival of St. Patrick. In those early ages there was no sugar, and honey was greatly valued, so that beehives were kept everywhere.

Ancient Irish bronze caldron for boiling meat, 12½ inches deep, formed of plates beautifully rivetted together. It shows marks and signs of long use over a fire. Now in the National Museum, Dublin.

Irish drinking vessel, called a Mether. They drank from the corners. At meals, the same mether was used by several persons, who drank from it in turn.

For drink, they had, besides plain water and milk, ale, and a sweet sort of liquor called mead both of which were made at home, and often wine, which was brought from the continent. There was then no whiskey.

In those days there were no hotels or inns as there are now, where a person could have board and lodging for payment; but they were not much needed then, as travelers were otherwise well provided for. Besides the monasteries, which, as we shall see further on, were always open and free to wayfarers, there were, all through the country, what were called "Houses of public hospitality." The keeper of one of those houses was called a *Brugaid* and sometimes a *Beetagh*; and his office was considered very high and honourable. A brugaid or beetagh had to keep an open house for travelers who were always welcome, and received bed and food free of charge. He was obliged by law to keep constantly in hands a large stock of provisions; and he should have a certain number of beds and all other

18

necessary household furniture. To enable a brugaid to keep up such an expensive establishment, he had the house itself and a large tract of land, free of rent and taxes, besides other liberal allowances.

The law required that there should be several open roads leading to the residence of every brugaid; and that a light should always be kept burning in the lawn at night to guide travelers to the house.

The people dressed well according to their means. Both men and women were fond of bright coloured garments, which were not hard to procure, as the art of dyeing in all the various hues was well understood.

It was usual for the same person to wear clothes of several brilliant colours: and sometimes the long outside mantle worn by men and women was striped and spotted with purple, yellow, green, or other dyes like Joseph's coat of many colours. Those who were able to afford it wore rings, bracelets, necklaces, gorgets, brooches, and other ornaments, made of gold, silver, and a sort of white bronze.

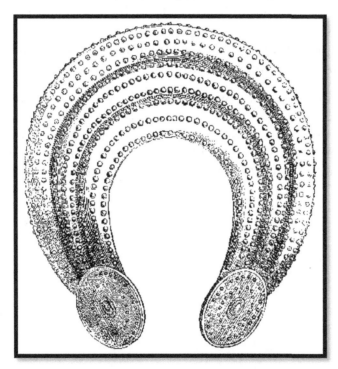

Ancient Irish Gorget for the neck: of gold, reddish in colour, and very pure: weighs 16⅓ oz. Now in the National Museum, Dublin.

The Irish metal workers were very skillful. They made brooches, rings, bracelets, croziers, crosses, and other such articles, in gold, silver, whitish bronze, gems, and enamel, of which many have been found in the earth from time to time, and are now kept in museums: and some of them are so skillfully and beautifully wrought that no artificer of the present day can imitate them.

There were men of the several professions, such as medical doctors, lawyers, judges, builders, poets, historians: and all through the country were to be found tradesmen of the various crafts—carpenters, smiths, workers in gold, silver, and brass, ship and boat builders, masons, shoemakers, dyers, tailors, brewers, and so-forth: all working industriously and earning their bread under the old Irish laws, which were everywhere acknowledged and obeyed. Then there was a good deal of commerce with Britain and with Continental countries, especially France; and the home commodities, such as hides, salt, wool, etc., were exchanged for wine, silk, satin, and other goods not produced in Ireland.

From what has been said here, we may see that the ancient Irish were orderly and regular in their way of life—quite on a level in this respect with the people of those other European countries of the same period that had a proper settled government; and, it will be shown further on in this book, that they were famed throughout all Europe for Religion and Learning.

The greatest evil of the country was war; for the kings and chiefs were very often fighting with each other, which brought great misery on the poor people where the disturbances took place. But in those early times war was common in all countries; and in this respect there was no more trouble in Ireland than in England, Scotland, and the countries of the Continent.

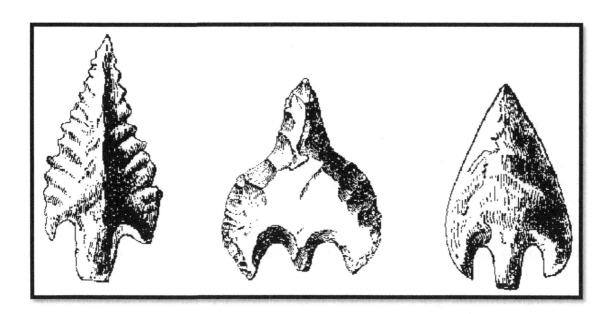

Flint arrow-heads. The head was fixed on the top of the shaft with cord of some kind, or with dried gut or tendon. Flint was used at a very early period when metals were either not known at all or were still very scarce. The makers of flint implements shaped them by chipping with stone hammers, in which they were very skillful and expert.

One form of Irish Ornament.

The Fate of the Children of Lir; or, The Four White Swans.

V.

HOW THE CHILDREN OF LIR WERE TURNED INTO SWANS.

During the time when the Dedannans ruled in Erin, there was a chief named Lir, who lived in Ulster, and who was much beloved for his goodness and his hospitality. He had four little children: a girl, named Finola, who was the eldest, and three boys, Aed, Ficra, and Conn: and Finola and Aed were twins, as were also Ficra and Conn. Their mother died when they were very young, and they were then placed in charge of one of Lir's friends named Eva, who was a witch-lady.

The four children grew up under Eva's care. She nursed them with great tenderness, and her love for them increased every day. They slept near their father; and he would often rise from his own bed at the dawn of morning, and go to their beds to talk with them and to fondle them. And they were the delight and joy of all the Dedannans, who often came to Lir's house to see them. For nowhere could four lovelier children be found; so that those who saw them were always delighted with their beauty and their gentleness, and could not help loving them with all their heart.

Now when Eva saw that the children of Lir received such attention and affection from all, she fancied she was neglected on their account; and a poisonous dart of jealousy entered her heart, which turned her love to hatred; and she began to have feelings of bitter enmity for the children.

Her jealousy so preyed on her that she feigned illness, and lay in bed for nearly a year, filled with gall and brooding mischief; and at the end of that time she committed a foul and cruel deed of treachery on the children of Lir.

One day she ordered her horses to be yoked to her chariot, and she set out for the palace of the Dedannan king, Bove Derg, bringing the four children with her. Finola did not wish to go, for it was revealed to her darkly in a dream that Eva was bent on some dreadful deed; and she knew well that the witch-lady intended to kill her and her brothers that day, or in some other way to bring ruin on them. But she was not able to avoid the fate that awaited her; so she went.

They fared on towards the palace, which was situated near Lough Derg in the south, till they came to the shore of Lake Darvra,[7] where they alighted; and the horses were unyoked. Eva led the children to the edge of the lake, and told them to go to bathe; and as soon as they had got into the clear water, she struck them one by one with a druidical fairy wand, and turned them into four beautiful snow-white swans. And she addressed them in these words—

Out to your home, ye swans, on Darvra's wave; With clamorous birds begin your life of gloom: Your friends shall weep your fate, but none can save; For I've pronounced the dreadful words of doom.

After this, the four children of Lir turned towards the witch-lady; and Finola spoke—

"Evil is the deed thou hast done, O Eva; thy friendship to us has been a friendship of treachery; and thou hast ruined us without cause. But the power of thy witchcraft is not greater than the druidical power of our friends to punish thee; and the doom that awaits thee shall be worse than ours."

The witch-lady loved us long ago; The witch-lady now has wrought us woe; With magical wand and fearful words, She changed us to beautiful snow-white birds; And we live on the waters for evermore, By tempests driven from shore to shore.

Finola again spoke and said, "Tell us now how long we shall be in the shape of swans, so that we may know when our miseries shall come to an end."

"It would be better for you if you had not put that question," said Eva; "but I will declare the truth to you, as you have asked me. Three hundred years on smooth Lake Darvra; three hundred years on the Sea of Moyle, between Erin and Alban;[8] three hundred years at Inish Glora[9] on the Western Sea. Until the union of Largnen, the prince from the north, with Decca, the princess from the south; until the Taillkenn[10] shall come to Erin, bringing the light of a pure faith; and until ye hear the voice of the Christian bell. And neither by your own power, nor by mine, nor by the power of your friends, can ye be freed till the time comes."

Then Eva repented what she had done; and she said, "Since I cannot afford you any other relief, I will allow you to keep your own Gaelic speech, and ye shall be able to sing sweet, plaintive fairy music, which shall excel all the music of the world, and which shall lull to sleep all that listen to it. Moreover, ye shall retain your human reason; and ye shall not be in grief on account of being in the shape of swans."

And she chanted this lay—

Depart from me, ye graceful swans; The waters are now your home: Your palace shall be the pearly cave, Your couch the crest of the crystal wave, And your mantle the milk-white foam!

Depart from me, ye snow-white swans, With your music and Gaelic speech: The crystal Darvra, the wintry Moyle, The billowy margin of Glora's isle;—Three hundred years on each!

Victorious Lir, your hapless sire, His loved ones in vain shall call; His weary heart is a husk of gore, His home is joyless for evermore, And his anger on me shall fall!

Through circling ages of gloom and fear Your anguish no tongue can tell; Till faith shall shed her heavenly rays, Till ye hear the Taillkenn's anthem of praise, And the voice of the Christian bell!

Then ordering her steeds to be yoked to her chariot, she set out once more for the palace leaving the four white swans swimming on the lake.

Our father shall watch and weep in vain; He never shall see us return again. Four pretty children, happy at home; Four white swans on the feathery foam; And we live on the waters for evermore, By tempests driven from shore to shore.

VI.

THE FOUR WHITE SWANS ON LAKE DARVRA.

Lir and his people, hearing that Eva had arrived at Bove Derg's palace without the children, became alarmed, and went southwards without delay; till passing by the shore of Lake Darvra, they saw the swans. And the swans swam up and spoke to them, at which they wondered greatly. But when they told Lir that they were indeed his four children whom the witch-lady had turned into birds, he and his people were struck with amazement and horror; and they uttered three long mournful cries of grief and lamentation. And when Lir had heard from Finola how the matter happened, he prepared to set out in quest of Eva. And bidding farewell to the children for a time, he chanted this lay:—

The time has come for me to part: No more, alas! my children dear, Your rosy smiles shall glad my heart, Or light the gloomy home of Lir.

Dark was the day when first I brought This Eva in my home to dwell! Hard was the woman's heart that wrought This cruel and malignant spell!

I lay me down to rest in vain; For, through the livelong, sleepless night, My little lov'd ones, pictured plain, Stand ever there before my sight.

Finola, once my pride and joy;Dark Aed, adventurous and bold; Bright Ficra, gentle, playful boy; And little Conn, with curls of gold;—

Struck down on Darvra's reedy shore, By wicked Eva's magic power: Oh, children, children, never more My heart shall know one peaceful hour.

After this he fared southwards till he arrived at the palace, where he found Eva. And the king, Bove Derg, when Lir had told him what Eva had done, was in great wrath; for he loved those little children. And calling Eva to him he spoke to her fiercely and asked her what shape of all others, on the earth, or above the earth, or beneath the earth, she most abhorred, and into which she most dreaded to be transformed.

And she, being forced to answer truly, said, "A demon of the air."

"That is the form you shall take," said Bove Derg; and as he spoke he struck Eva with a druidical magic wand, and turned her into a demon of the air. She opened her wings, and flew with a scream upwards and away through the clouds; and she is still a demon of the air, and she shall be a demon of the air till the end of time.

After this, Lir and the Dedannans came to live on the shore of the lake, to be near the swans and to speak with them. And so the swans passed their time on the waters. During the day they discoursed lovingly with their father and their friends; and at night they chanted their slow, sweet, fairy music, the most delightful that was ever heard by men; so that all who listened to it, even those who were in grief, or sickness, or pain, forgot their sorrows and their sufferings, and fell into a gentle, sweet sleep from which they awoke bright and happy. At last the three hundred years[11] came to an end, and Finola said to her brothers:—

"Do you know, my dear brothers, that we have come to the end of our time here; and that we have only this one night to spend on Lake Darvra?"

When the three sons of Lir heard this, they were in great distress and sorrow; for they were almost as happy on Lake Darvra, surrounded by their friends, and conversing with them day by day, as if they had been in their father's house in their own natural shapes; whereas they should now live on the gloomy and tempest-tossed Sea of Moyle, far away from all human society.

Early next morning, the swans came to the margin of the lake to speak to their father and their friends for the last time, and to bid them farewell; and Finola chanted this lay—

I.

Farewell, farewell, our father dear! The last sad hour has come: Farewell, Bove Derg! farewell to all, Till the dreadful day of doom! We go from friends and scenes beloved, To a home of grief and pain; And that day of woe Shall come and go, Before we meet again!

II.

We live for ages on stormy Moyle, In loneliness and fear; The kindly words of loving friends We never more shall hear. Four joyous children long ago; Four snow-white swans to-day; And on Moyle's wild sea Our robe shall be The cold and briny spray.

III.

Far down on the misty stream of time, When three hundred years are o'er, Three hundred more in storm and cold, By Glora's desolate shore; Till Decca fair is Largnen's spouse; Till north and south unite; Till the hymns are sung, And the bells are rung, At the dawn of the pure faith's light.

IV.

Arise, my brothers, from Darvra's wave On the wings of the southern wind; We leave our father and friends to-day In measureless grief behind.[Pg 32]Ah! sad the parting, and sad our flight To Moyle's tempestuous main; For the day of woe Shall come and go, Before we meet again!

The four swans then spread their wings, and rose from the surface of the water in sight of all their friends, till they reached a great height in the air; then resting, and looking downwards for a moment, they flew straight to the north, till they alighted on the Sea of Moyle between Erin and Alban.

VII.

THE FOUR WHITE SWANS ON THE SEA OF MOYLE.

Miserable was the abode and evil the plight of the children of Lir on the Sea of Moyle. Their hearts were wrung with sorrow for their father and their friends; and when they looked towards the steep rocky, far-stretching coasts, and saw the great, dark, wild sea around them, they were overwhelmed with fear and despair. They began also to suffer from cold and hunger, so that all the hardships they had endured on Lake Darvra appeared as nothing compared with their suffering on the sea-current of Moyle.[Pg 33]

And so they lived, till one night a great tempest fell upon the sea. Finola, when she saw the sky filled with black, threatening clouds, thus addressed her brothers:—

"Beloved brothers, we have made a bad preparation for this night: for it is certain that the coming storm will separate us; and now let us appoint a place of meeting, or it may happen that we shall never see each other again."

And they answered, "Dear sister, you speak truly and wisely; and let us fix on Carricknarone,[12] for that is a rock that we are all very well acquainted with."

And they appointed Carricknarone as their place of meeting.

Midnight came, and with it came the beginning of the storm. A wild, rough wind swept over the dark sea, the lightnings flashed, and the great waves rose, and increased their violence and their thunder.

The swans were soon scattered over the waters, so that not one of them knew in what direction the others had been driven. During all that night they were tossed about by the roaring winds and waves, and it was with much difficulty they preserved their lives.

Towards morning the storm abated, the sky cleared, and the sea became again calm and smooth; and Finola swam to Carricknarone. But she found[Pg 34]none of her brothers there, neither could she see any trace of them when she looked all round from the summit of the rock over the wide face of the sea.

Then she became terrified, thinking she should never see them again; and she began to lament them plaintively.

[On this incident Thomas Moore wrote the following beautiful song. A person is supposed to be listening to Finola, and—in the first four lines of the song—calls on the winds and the waves to be silent that he may hear.]

SILENT, O MOYLE!

Silent, O Moyle! be the roar of thy water, Break not, ye breezes! your chain of repose, While, murmuring mournfully, Lir's lonely daughter Tells to the night-star her tale of woes. When shall the Swan, her death-note singing, Sleep with wings in darkness furl'd? When will Heav'n, its sweet bell ringing, Call my spirit from this stormy world?

Sadly, O Moyle! to thy winter-wave weeping, Fate bids me languish long ages away; Yet still in her darkness doth Erin lie sleeping Still doth the pure light its dawning delay When will that day-star, mildly springing, Warm our Isle with peace and love? When will Heaven, its sweet bell ringing, Call my spirit to the fields above?

At last, while she stood gazing in despair over the waste of waters, she saw her brothers swimming from different directions towards the rock. They came to her one by one, and she welcomed them joyfully: and she placed Aed under the feathers of her breast, and Ficra and Conn under her wings, and said to them:— "My dear brothers, though ye may think last night very bad, we shall have many like it from this time forth."

So they continued for a long time on the Sea of Moyle, suffering hardships of every kind, till one winter night came upon them, of great wind and of snow and frost so severe, that nothing they ever before suffered could be compared to the misery of that night. The swans remained on Carricknarone, and their feet and their wings were frozen to the icy surface, so that they had to strive hard to move from their places in the morning; and they left the skin of their feet, the quills of their wings, and the feathers of their breasts clinging to the rock.

"Sad is our condition this night, my beloved brothers," said Finola, "for we are forbidden to leave the Sea of Moyle; and yet we cannot bear the salt water, for when it enters our wounds, I fear we shall die of pain." And she uttered these words—

Our life is a life of woe; No shelter or rest we find: How bitterly drives the snow; How cold is this wintry wind!

From the icy spray of the sea, From the wind of the bleak north-east, I shelter my brothers three, Under my wings and breast.

The witch-lady sent us here, And misery well we know:—In cold and hunger and fear; Our life is a life of woe![13]

They were, however, forced to swim out on the stream of Moyle, all wounded and torn as they were; for though the brine was sharp and bitter, they were not able to avoid it. They stayed as near the coast as they could, till after a long time the feathers of their breasts and wings grew again, and their wounds were healed.

After this the swans lived on for a great number of years, sometimes visiting the shores of Erin, and sometimes the headlands of Alban. But they always returned to the sea-stream of Moyle, for it was to be their home till the end of three hundred years.

One day they came to the mouth of the Bann, on the north coast of Erin, and looking inland, they saw a stately troop of horsemen approaching directly from the south-west. They were mounted on white steeds, and clad in bright-coloured garments, and as they wound towards the shore their arms glittered in the sun.

These were a party of the Dedannans who had been a long time searching for the children of Lir along the northern shores of Erin: and now that they had found them, they were joyful; and they and the swans greeted each other with tender expressions of friendship and love. The children of Lir inquired after the Dedannans, and particularly after their father Lir; and for Bove Derg, and for all the rest of their friends and acquaintances.

"They are well," replied the Dedannans; "but all are mourning for you since the day you left Lake Darvra. And now we wish to know how you fare on this wild sea."

"Miserable has been our life since that day," said Finola; "and no tongue can tell the suffering and sorrow we have endured on the Sea of Moyle." And she chanted these words—

Ah, happy is Lir's bright home to-day, With mead and music and poet's lay: But gloomy and cold his children's home, Forever tossed on the briny foam.

Our wreathèd feathers are thin and light When the wind blows keen through the wintry night: Yet often we were robed, long, long ago, In purple mantles and furs of snow.

On Moyle's bleak current our food and wine Are sandy sea-weed and bitter brine: Yet oft we feasted in days of old, And hazel-mead drank from cups of gold.

Our beds are rocks in the dripping caves ;Our lullaby song the roar of the waves: But soft rich couches once we pressed, And harpers lulled us each night to rest.

Lonely we swim on the billowy main, Through frost and snow, through storm and rain: Alas for the days when round us moved The chiefs and princes and friends we loved!

My little twin brothers beneath my wings Lie close when the north wind bitterly stings, And Aed close nestles before my breast; Thus side by side through the night we rest.

Our father's fond kisses, Bove Derg's embrace, The light of Mannanan's godlike face ,The love of Angus—all, all are o'er; And we live on the billows for evermore!

After this they bade each other farewell, for it was not permitted to the children of Lir to remain away from the stream of Moyle.

VIII.

HOW THE CHILDREN OF LIR REGAINED THEIR HUMAN SHAPE AND DIED.

Great was the misery of the Children of Lir on the sea of Moyle till their three hundred years were ended. Then Finola said to her brothers—

"It is time for us to leave this place, for our period here has come to an end."

The hour has come; the hour has come; Three hundred years have passed: We leave this bleak and gloomy home, And we fly to the west at last!

We leave forever the stream of Moyle; On the clear, cold wind we go; Three hundred years round Glora's Isle, Where wintry tempests blow!

No sheltered home, no place of rest, From the tempest's angry blast: Fly, brothers, fly, to the distant west, For the hour has come at last!

So the swans left the Sea of Moyle, and flew westward, till they reached the sea round the Isle of Glora. There they remained for three[Pg 40]hundred years, suffering much from storm and cold, and in nothing better off than they were on the Sea of Moyle. Towards the end of that time, St. Patrick came to Erin with the pure faith; and St. Kemoc, one of his companions, came to Inish Glora. The first night Kemoc came to the island, the children of Lir heard his bell at early matin time, ringing faintly in the distance. And the three sons of Lir trembled with fear, for the sound was strange and dreadful to them. But Finola knew well what it was; and she soothed them and said:—"My dear brothers, this is the voice of the Christian bell: and now the end of our suffering is near: for this bell is the signal that we shall soon be freed from our spell, and released from our life of suffering; for God has willed it."

And when the bell ceased she chanted this lay—

Listen, ye swans, to the voice of the bell, The sweet bell we've dreamed of for many a year; Its tones floating by on the night breezes, tell That the end of our long life of sorrow is near!

Listen, ye swans, to the heavenly strain; 'Tis the anchoret tolling his soft matin bell: He has come to release us, from sorrow, from pain, From the cold and tempestuous shores where we dwell!

Trust in the glorious Lord of the sky; He will free us from Eva's druidical spell: Be thankful and glad, for our freedom is nigh, And listen with joy to the voice of the bell!

"Let us sing our music now," said Finola.

And they chanted a low, sweet, plaintive strain of fairy music, to praise and thank the great high King of heaven and earth.

Kemoc heard the music from where he stood; and he listened with great astonishment. And he came and spoke to the swans, and asked them were they the children of Lir. They replied, "We are indeed the children of Lir, who were changed long ago into swans by the spells of the witch-lady."

"I give God thanks that I have found you," said Kemoc; "for it is on your account I have come to this little island." Then he brought them to his own house; and, sending for a skillful workman, he caused him to make two bright, slender chains of silver; and he put a chain between Finola and Aed, and the other chain he put between Ficra and Conn. And there they lived with Kemoc in content and happiness.

Now there was in that place a certain king named Largnen, whose queen was Decca: the very king and queen whom the witch-lady had foretold on the day when she changed the children into swans, nine hundred years before. And Queen Decca, hearing[Pg 42]all about those wonderful speaking swans, wished to have them for herself: so she sent to Kemoc for them; but he refused to give them. Whereupon the queen waxed very wroth: and her husband the king, when she told him about it, was wroth also: and he set out straightway for Kemoc's house to

31

bring the swans away by force. The swans were at this time standing in the little church with Kemoc. And Largnen coming up, seized the two silver chains, one in each hand, and drew the birds towards the door; while Kemoc followed him, much alarmed lest they should be injured.

The king had proceeded only a little way, when suddenly the white feathery robes faded and disappeared; and the swans regained their human shape, Finola being transformed into an extremely old woman, and the three sons into three feeble old men, white-haired and bony and wrinkled.

When the king saw this, he started with affright, and instantly left the place without speaking one word.

As to the children of Lir, they turned towards Kemoc; and Finola spoke—

"Come, holy cleric, and baptize us without delay, for our death is near. You will grieve after us, O Kemoc; but in truth you are not more sorrowful at parting from us than we are at parting from you. Make our grave here and bury us together; and as I often sheltered my brothers when we were swans, so[Pg 43]let us be placed in the grave—Conn standing near me at my right side, Ficra at my left, and Aed before my face."[14]

Come, holy priest, with book and prayer Baptize and bless us here: Haste, cleric, haste, for the hour has come And death at last is near!

Dig our grave—a deep, deep grave, Near the church we loved so well; This little church, where first we heard The voice of the Christian bell.

As oft in life my brothers dear Were sooth'd by me to rest—Ficra and Conn beneath my wings, And Aed before my breast;

So place the two on either hand—Close, like the love that bound me; Place Aed as close before my face, And twine their arms around me

Thus shall we rest for evermore, My brothers dear and I; Haste, cleric, haste, baptize and bless, For death at last is nigh!

Then the children of Lir were baptized, and they died immediately. And when they died, Kemoc looked up; and lo, he saw a vision of four lovely children, with light, silvery wings, and faces all radiant with joy. They gazed on him for a moment; but even as they gazed, they vanished upwards, and he saw them no more. And he was filled with gladness, for he knew they had gone to heaven; but when he looked down on the four bodies lying before him, he became sad and wept.

And Kemoc caused a wide and deep grave to be dug near the little church; and the children of Lir were buried together, as Finola had directed—Conn at her right hand, Ficra at her left, and Aed standing before her face. And he raised a grave-mound over them, placing a tombstone on it, with their names graved in Ogham;[15] after which he uttered a lament for them, and their funeral rites were performed.

So far we have related the sorrowful story of the Fate of the Children of Lir.

From "Old Celtic Romances," by P. W. JOYCE, LL.D.

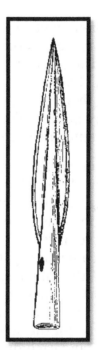

Bronze spear-head. A long handle was fixed in the socket and fastened by a rivet.

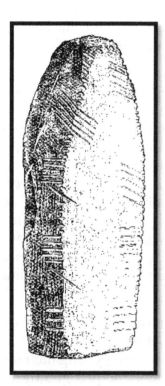

An Ogham stone.

Bronze sword. A hilt was fixed on by rivets.

IX.

HOW RELIGION AND LEARNING FLOURISHED IN IRELAND.

As soon as St. Patrick had entered on his mission in Ireland, he began to found monasteries, which continued to spread through every part of the country for hundreds of years after his time. Though religion was their main object, these establishments were among the chief means of spreading general[Pg 46]enlightenment among the people. Almost every monastery had a school or college attached, at the head of which was some man who was a great scholar and teacher. The teachers were generally monks: but many learned laymen were also employed. Some colleges had very large numbers of students: for instance, we are told that there were 3000 in each of the two colleges of Clonard and Bangor[16]; and many others might be named, which, though not so large, had yet several hundred students in each.

In these monasteries and their schools all was life and activity. The monks were always busily employed; some at tillage on the farm round the monastery—ploughing, digging, sowing, reaping—some teaching, others writing books. The duty of a few was to attend to travelers, to wash their feet and prepare supper and bed for them: for strangers who called at the monastery were always received with welcome, and got lodging, food, and attendance from the monks, all free. Others of the inmates, again, employed themselves in cooking, or carpentry, or smith work, or making clothes, for the use of the community. Besides all this they had their devotions to attend to, at certain times, both day and night, throughout the year. As for the students, they had to mind their own[Pg 47]simple household concerns, and each day when these were finished they had plenty of employment in their studies: for the professors kept them hard at work.

There were also great numbers of schools not held in monasteries, conducted by laymen, some for general learning, such as History, Poetry, Grammar, Latin, Greek, Irish, the Sciences, &c.; and some for teaching and training young men for professions, such as lawyers and doctors. And these schools helped greatly to spread learning, though they were not so well known outside Ireland as the monastic schools.

The Irish professors were so famed for their learning, and the colleges were so excellent, that students came to them from every country of Europe: but more from Great Britain than elsewhere. The Irish were very much pleased to receive these foreign students: and they were so generous that they supplied them with food, gave them the manuscript books they wanted to learn from, and taught them too, all free of charge. Ireland was in those times the most learned country in Europe, so that it was known by the name of the Island of Saints and Scholars.

But the Irish scholars and missionaries did not confine themselves to their own country. Great numbers of them went abroad—to Britain and elsewhere—to teach and to preach the Gospel to the people. The professors from Ireland were held in such estimation that they were employed to teach in[Pg 48]most of the schools and colleges of Great Britain and the Continent.

We shall see that the Northern Picts of Scotland were converted by St. Columkille and his monks from Iona: and a large proportion of the people of England became Christians through the preaching of Irish monks before the arrival of St. Augustine.[17]

The Irish missionaries, who went to the Continent, in their eagerness to spread religion and knowledge, penetrated to all parts of Europe: they even found their way to Iceland. Few people have any idea of the trials and dangers they encountered. Most of them were persons in good position, who might have lived in plenty and comfort at home. They knew well, when setting out, that they were leaving country and friends probably forever: for of those that went, very few ever returned. Once on the Continent, they had to make their way poor and friendless, through people whose language they did not understand, and who were in many places ten times more rude and dangerous in those ages than the inhabitants of these islands: and we know, as a matter of history, that many were killed on the way. Then these earnest men had, of course, to learn the language of the people among whom they[Pg 49]took up their abode: for until they did this they had to employ an interpreter, which was a very troublesome and slow way of preaching. But the noble-hearted missionaries went forth to do their good work; and no labours, hardships, or dangers could turn them from their purpose.

More than three hundred years ago the great English poet, Edmund Spenser, lived some time in Ireland, and made himself very well acquainted with its history. He knew what kind of a country it was in past ages; so that in one of his poems he speaks of the time

"When Ireland florishèd in fame Of wealth and goodness, far above the rest Of all that beare the British Islands name."

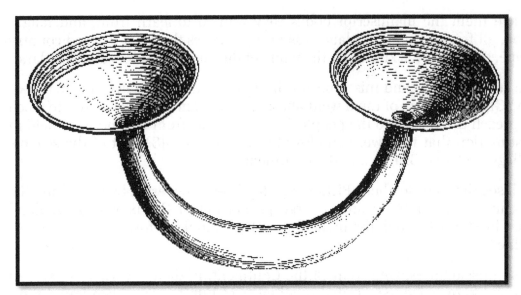

Ancient Irish solid gold ornament, now in the National Museum Dublin. It is double the size of the picture, and weighs 5¼ oz. Great numbers of gold objects, shaped like this, are in the National Museum, some very large—one of them weighing 33 oz.: while others are quite small, not bigger than a common coat-button. Besides being ornaments, it is believed that they were used as money, as there were no coins in use in very ancient times in Ireland.

X.

THE RED BRANCH KNIGHTS.

Nearly two miles west of Armagh are the remains of the ancient palace of Emain, or Emain Macha, often called Emania. They consist of a great circular *rath* or rampart of earth, with a deep trench outside it, and a high mound within, the whole structure covering a space of about thirteen acres. At one time the circular ring was complete, but of late years some portions of it have been leveled or removed. The houses in which the kings and heroes of old, with their numerous households, lived and feasted, stood mostly within the enclosure, and were all of wood, not a trace of which remains. This great fort is now called by the people of the place, the "Navan Fort," or "Navan Ring."

According to Irish legendary history, Emain was founded about three centuries before the beginning of the Christian era, by Macha of the Golden Hair, queen of Ulster; and for more than six hundred years it was the residence of the kings of that province. But about the year A.D. 331, it was destroyed by three princes from Tara, who invaded and conquered that part of Ulster; after which Emain was no longer inhabited.

Early in the first century of the Christian era flourished the Red Branch Knights, a band of heroes in the service of Concobar (or Conor) Mac Nessa, king of Ulster. There were several bodies of them, under separate commanders, who lived in different parts of the province. These leaders were the great heroes of the Red Branch, who are celebrated in ancient Irish romance, and who are mentioned by Moore in his song, "Let Erin remember":—

"When her kings with standard of green unfurled Led the Red Branch Knights to danger."

Every year during the summer months, various companies of the Knights came to Emain under their several commanders, to be drilled and trained in military science and feats of arms. They were lodged in a large separate building beside Emain, called Creeveroe or the Red Branch—from which the whole force took its name: and the townland in which this great house stood is still called Creeveroe. Each day the leaders were feasted by King Concobar Mac Nessa in his own banqueting hall at Emain.

The greatest of all the Red Branch heroes was Cu-Culainn—"the mightiest hero of the Scots," as he is called in one of the oldest of the Irish books—whose residence was *Dundalgan*, a mile west of the present town of Dundalk. This dun or fort consists of a high mound surrounded by an earthen rampart[Pg 52]and trench,

37

all of immense size, even in their ruined state; but it has lost its old name and is now called the Moat of Castletown, while the original name Dundalgan, slightly altered, has been transferred to Dundalk.

Another of these Red Branch Knights' residences stands beside Downpatrick: viz., the great fort anciently called (among other names) Dun-Keltair or Rath-Keltair, where lived the hero, Keltar of the Battles. It consists of a huge embankment of earth, nearly circular, with the usual deep trench outside it, covering a space of about ten acres.

Next to Cuculainn, the most renowned of those knights were Fergus Mac Roy, Leary the Victorious, Conall Carnagh, and the three Sons of Usna.

There were, at this same time, similar orders of knights in the other provinces. Those of Munster were commanded by Curoi Mac Dara, who lived in a great stone fortress high up on the side of Caherconree Mountain, near Tralee, the remains of which may be seen to this day. He was a mighty champion, and on one occasion vanquished Cuculainn in single combat. The Connaught knights were in the service of Maive, the warlike queen of that province, whose residence was the palace of Croghan, the ruins of which still remain near the village of Rathcroghan in the north of Roscommon.

In the Book of the Dun Cow, the Book of Leinster, and other old manuscripts (which will be found described farther on), there are great numbers of romantic stories about those Red Branch Knights, and about the Knights of Munster and Connaught, of which many have been translated and published.

The most celebrated of all these tales is what is called the *Tain* or "Cattle spoil" of Quelna or Cooley.[18] Queen Maive, having some cause of quarrel with an Ulster chief, set out with her army for the north on a plundering expedition, attended by all the great heroes of Connaught. During the march northwards, the queen, as the story tells us, had nine splendid chariots for herself and her attendant chiefs, her own in the centre, with two abreast in front, two behind, and two on each side, right and left; and—in the words of the old tale—"the reason for this order was, lest the clods from the hoofs of the horses, or the foam-flakes from their mouths, or the dust raised by that mighty host, should strike and tarnish the golden diadem on the head of the queen."

The invading army entered Quelna, which was then a part of Ulster and belonged to Cuculainn. It happened just then that the men of Ulster were under a spell of feebleness, all but Cuculainn, who had to defend single-handed the several fords and passes, in a series of combats against Maive's best champions, in all of which he was victorious. But, in spite of what he could do, Queen Maive carried off nearly all the best cattle of Quelna, and, at their head, a great brown bull which indeed was what she chiefly came for. At length the Ulstermen, having been freed from the spell, attacked and routed the Connaught army. The battles, single combats, and other incidents of this war are related in the Tain, which consists of one main story, with about thirty minor tales grouped round it. Another Red Branch story is the Fate of the Sons of Usna, which has been always a favourite with Irish story-tellers, and with the Irish people in general, and which is now given here, translated in full.

A "Cromlech," an ancient Irish tomb: still to be seen in its place in the Phœnix Park, Dublin. This is rather a small one, the covering stone being only about 6½ feet long. Some cromlechs are very large: one at Kilternan near Dublin has a covering stone 23½ feet long, 17 feet broad, and 6½ feet thick: and no one can tell how the people of old lifted it up.

Deirdre; or, The Fate of the Sons of Usna.

XI.

THE FLIGHT TO ALBAN.

Concobar Mac Nessa king of Ulaid[20] ruled in Emain. And his chief storyteller, Felimid, made a feast for the king and for the knights of the Red Branch; who all came to partake of it in his house. While they were feasting right joyously, listening to the sweet music of the harps and the mellow voices of the bards, a messenger brought word that Felimid's wife had given birth to a little daughter, an infant of wondrous beauty. And when Caffa, the king's druid and seer, who was of the company, was aware of the birth of the child, he went forth to view the stars and the clouds, if he might thereby glean knowledge of what was in store for that little babe.[21] And when he had returned to his place, he sat deep pondering for a time: and then standing up and obtaining silence, he said:—

"This child shall be called Deir-drĕ[22]; and fittingly is she so named: for much of woe will befal Ulaid and Erin in general on her account. There shall be jealousies, and strifes, and wars: evil deeds will be done: many heroes will be exiled: many will fall."

When the heroes heard this they were sorely troubled, and some said that the child should be killed. But the king said:—"Not so, ye Knights of the Red Branch, it is not meet to commit a base deed in order to escape evils that may never come to pass. This little maid shall be reared out of the reach of mischief, and when she is old enough she shall be my wife: thus shall I be the better able to guard against those evils that Caffa forecasts for us."

And the Ultonians did not dare to gainsay the word of the king.

Then king Concobar caused the child to be placed in a strong fortress on a lonely spot nigh the palace, with no opening in front, but with door and windows looking out at the back on a lovely garden watered by a clear rippling stream: and house and garden were surrounded by a wall that no man could surmount. And those who were put in charge of her were, her tutor, and her nurse, and Concobar's[Pg 57]poetess, whose name was Lavarcam: and save these three, none were permitted to see her. And so she grew up in this solitude, year by year, till she was of marriageable age; when she excelled all the maidens of her time for beauty.

40

One snowy day as she and Lavarcam looked forth from the window, they saw some blood on the snow, where her tutor had killed a calf for dinner; and a raven alighted and began to drink of it. "I should like," said Deirdre, "that he who is to be my husband should have these three colours: his hair as black as the raven: his cheeks red as the blood: his skin like the snow. And I saw such a youth in a dream last night; but I know not where he is, or whether he is living on the ridge of the world."

"Truly," said Lavarcam, "the young hero that answers to thy words is not far from thee; for he is among Concobar's knights: namely, Naisi the son of Usna."

Now Naisi and his brothers, Ainnli and Ardan, the three Sons of Usna, were the best beloved of all the Red Branch Knights, so gracious and gentle were they in time of peace, so skillful and swift-footed in the chase, so strong and valiant in battle.

And when Deirdre heard Lavarcam's words, she said:—"If it be as thou sayest, that this young knight is near us, I shall not be happy till I see him: and I beseech thee to bring him to speak to me."[Pg 58]

"Alas, child," replied Lavarcam, "thou knowest not the peril of what thou askest me to do: for if thy tutor come to know of it, he will surely tell the king; and the king's anger none can bear."

Deirdre answered not: but she remained for many days sad and silent: and her eyes often filled with tears through memory of her dream: so that Lavarcam was grieved: and she pondered on the thing if it could be done, for she loved Deirdre very much and had compassion on her. At last she contrived that these two should meet without the tutor's knowledge: and the end of the matter was that they loved each other: and Deirdre said she would never wed the king, but she would wed Naisi.

Knowing well the doom that awaited them when Concobar came to hear of this, Naisi and his young wife and his two brothers, with thrice fifty fighting men, thrice fifty women, thrice fifty attendants, and thrice fifty hounds, fled over sea to Alban. And the king of the western part of Alban received them kindly and took them into military service. Here they remained for a space, gaining daily in favour: but they kept Deirdre apart, fearing evil if the king should see her.

And so matters went on, till it chanced that the king's steward, coming one day by Naisi's house, saw the couple as they sat on their couch: and going directly to his master, he said:—

"O king, we have long sought in vain for a[Pg 59]woman worthy to be thy wife, and now at last we have found her: for the woman, Deirdre, who is with Naisi, is worthy to be the wife of the king of the western world. And now I give thee this counsel:—Let Naisi be killed, and then take thou Deirdre for thy wife."

A burial urn. The ancient Irish sometimes buried as we do now, placing the body in the grave, over which they often raised a cairn or a cromlech. Sometimes they burned the body and put the ashes in an urn, which they placed under a cromlech, or cairn, or burial mound. Urns were always made of clay, which was baked till it was hard. They are often found in graves, especially under cairns and cromlechs: and they nearly always contain ashes and bits of burnt bones. Occasionally, as has been already said persons were buried standing up, especially kings and warriors, who were placed in the grave fully armed.

The king basely agreed to do so; and forthwith he laid a plot to slay the sons of Usna; which matter coming betimes to the ears of the brothers, they fled by night with all their people. And when they had got to a safe distance, they took up their abode in a wild place, where with much ado they obtained food[Pg 60]by hunting and fishing. And the brothers built them three hunting booths in the forest, a little distance from that part of the seashore looking towards Erin: and the booth in which their food was prepared, in that they did not eat; and the one in which they ate, in that they did not sleep. And their people in like manner built themselves booths and huts, which gave them but scant shelter from wind and weather.

Now when it came to the ears of the Ultonians, that the sons of Usna and their people were in discomfort and danger, they were sorely grieved: but they kept their thoughts to themselves, for they dared not speak their mind to the king.

XII.

CONCOBAR'S GUILEFUL MESSAGE.

At this same time a right joyous and very splendid feast was driven by Concobar in Emain Macha to the nobles and the knights of his household. And the number of the king's household that sat them down in the great hall of Emain on that occasion was five and three score above six hundred and one thousand.[23] Then arose, in turn, their musicians to[Pg 61]sound their melodious harp strings, and their poets and their story-tellers to sing their sweet poetic strains, and to recount the deeds of the mighty heroes of the olden time. And the feasting and the enjoyment went on, and the entire assembly were gay and cheerful. At length Concobar arose from where he sat high up on his royal seat; whereupon the noise of mirth was instantly hushed. And he raised his kingly voice and said:—

"I desire to know from you, ye Nobles and Knights of the Red Branch, have you ever seen in any quarter of Erin, a house better than this house of Emain, which is my mansion: and whether you see any want in it."

And they answered that they saw no better house, and that they knew of no want in it.

And the king said: "I know of a great want: namely, that we have not present among us the three noble sons of Usna. And why now should they be in banishment on account of any woman in the world?"

And the nobles replied:—"Truly it is a sad thing that the sons of Usna, our dear comrades, should be in exile and distress. They were a shield of defence to Ulaid: and now, O king, it will please us well that thou send for them and bring them back, lest they and their people perish by famine or fall by their enemies."

"Let them come," replied Concobar, "and make[Pg 62]submission to me: and their homes, and their lands, and their places among the Knights of the Red Branch shall be restored to them."

Now Concobar was mightily enraged at the marriage and flight of Naisi and Deirdre, though he hid his mind from all men; and he spoke these words pretending forgiveness and friendship. But there was guile in his heart, and he planned to allure them back to Ulaid that he might kill them.

When the feast was ended, and the company had departed, the king called unto him Fergus Mac Roy, and said:—"Go thou, Fergus, and bring back the sons of Usna and their people. I promise thee that I will receive them as friends should be received, and that what awaits them here is not enmity or injury, but welcome and friendship. Take my message of peace and good will, and give thyself as pledge and surety for their safety. But these two things I charge thee to do:—That the moment you land in Ulaid on your way back, you proceed straight to Barach's house which stands on the sea cliff high over the landing place fronting Alban: and that whether the time of your arrival be by day or by night, thou see that the sons of Usna tarry not, but let them come hither direct to Emain, that they may not eat food in Erin till they eat of mine."

And Fergus, suspecting no evil design, promised to do as the king directed: for he was glad to be sent on this errand, being a fast friend to the sons of Usna.[Pg 63]

Fergus set out straightway, bringing with him only his two sons, Illan the Fair and Buinni the Red, and his shield bearer to carry his shield. And as soon as he had departed, Concobar sent for Barach and said to him:—

"Prepare a feast in thy house for Fergus: and when he visits thee returning with the sons of Usna, invite him to partake of it." And Barach thereupon departed for his home to do the bidding of the king and prepare the feast.

Now those heroes of old, on the day they received knighthood, were wont to make certain pledges which were to bind them for life, some binding themselves to one thing, some to another. And as they made the promises on the faith of their knighthood, with great vows, in presence of kings and nobles, they dared not violate them; no, not even if it was to save the lives of themselves and all their friends: for whosoever broke through his knighthood pledge was foully dishonoured for evermore. And one of Fergus's obligations was never to refuse an

44

invitation to a banquet: a thing which was well known to King Concobar and to Barach.

As to Fergus Mac Roy and his sons: they went on board their galley and put to sea, and made no delay till they reached the harbour nigh the campment of the sons of Usna. And coming ashore, Fergus gave the loud shout of a mighty man of chase. The sons of Usna were at that same hour in their booth; and[Pg 64]Naisi and Deirdre were sitting with a polished chessboard between them playing a game.

And when they heard the shout, Naisi said:—"That is the call of a man from Erin."

"Not so," replied Deirdre, "it is the call of a man of Alban."

And after a little time when a second shout came, Naisi said:—"That of a certainty is the call of a man of Erin!"

But Deirdre again replied:—"No, indeed: it concerns us not: let us play our game."

But when a third shout came sounding louder than those before, Naisi arose and said:—"Now I know the voice: that is the shout of Fergus!" And straightway he sent Ardan to the shore to meet him.

Now Deirdre knew the voice of Fergus from the first: but she kept her thoughts to herself: for her heart misgave her that the visit boded evil. And when she told Naisi that she knew the first shout, he said:—"Why, my queen, didst thou conceal it then?"

And she replied:—"Lo, I saw a vision in my sleep last night: three birds came to us from Emain Macha, with three drops of honey in their beaks, and they left us the honey and took away three drops of our blood."

"What dost thou read from that vision, O princess?" said Naisi.[Pg 65]

"It denotes the message from Concobar to us," said Deirdre; "for sweet as honey is the message of peace from a false man, while he has thoughts of blood hidden deep in his heart."

When Ardan arrived at the shore, the sight of Fergus and his two sons was to him like rain on the parched grass; for it was long since he had seen any of his dear comrades from Erin. And he cried out as he came near, "An affectionate welcome to you my dear companions": and he fell on Fergus's neck and kissed his cheeks, and did the like to his sons. Then he brought them to the hunting-booth; and

Naisi, Ainnli, and Deirdre gave them a like kind welcome; after which they asked the news from Erin.

"The best news I have," said Fergus, "is that Concobar has sent me to you with kindly greetings, to bring you back to Emain and restore you to your lands and homes, and to your places in the Red Branch; and I am myself a pledge for your safety."

"It is not meet for them to go," said Deirdre: "for here they are under no man's rule; and their sway in Alban is even as great as the sway of Concobar in Erin."

But Fergus said: "One's mother country is better than all else, and gloomy is life when a man sees not his home each morning."

"Far dearer to me is Erin than Alban," said Naisi, "even though my sway should be greater here."

It was not with Deirdre's consent he spoke these words: and she still earnestly opposed their return to Erin.

But Fergus tried to re-assure her:—"If all the men of Erin were against you," said he, "it would avail nought once I have passed my word for your safety."

"We trust in thee," said Naisi, "and we will go with thee to Erin."

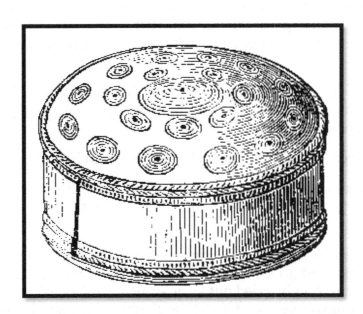

A gold box: 2¾ inches across: 1 inch deep. Found in a grave in Co.

Cork. Use not known.

XIII.

THE RETURN TO EMAIN.

Going next morning on board their galleys, Fergus and his companions put out on the wide sea: and oar and wind bore them on swiftly till they landed on the shore of Erin near the house of Barach.[Pg 67]

And Deirdre, seating herself on a cliff, looked sadly over the waters at the blue headlands of Alban: and she uttered this farewell:—

I.

"Dear to me is yon eastern land: Alban with its wonders. Beloved is Alban with its bright harbours and its pleasant hills of the green slopes. From that land I would never depart except to be with Naisi.

II.

Kil-Cuan, O Kil-Cuan,[24] whither Ainnli was wont to resort: short seemed the time to me while I sojourned there with Naisi on the margins of its streams and waterfalls.

III.

"Glen-Lee, O Glen-Lee, where I slept happy under soft coverlets: fish and fowl, and the flesh of red deer and badgers; these were our fare in Glen-Lee.

IV.

"Glen-Masan, O Glen-Masan: tall its cresses of white stalks: often were we rocked to sleep in our curragh in the grassy harbour of Glen-Masan.

V.

"Glen-Orchy, O Glen-Orchy: over thy straight glen rises the smooth ridge that oft echoed to the voices of our hounds. No man of the clan was more light-hearted than my Naisi when following the chase in Glen-Orchy.

VI.

"Glen-Ettive, O Glen-Ettive: there it was that my first house was raised for me: lovely its woods in the smile of the early morn: the sun loves to shine on Glen-Ettive.

VII.

"Glen-da-Roy, O Glen-da-Roy: the memory of its people is dear to me: sweet is the cuckoo's note from the bending bough on the peak over Glen-da-Roy.

VIII.

"Dear to me is Dreenagh over the resounding shore: dear to me its crystal waters over the speckled sand. From those sweet places I would never depart, but only to be with my beloved Naisi."

After this they entered the house of Barach; and when Barach had welcomed them, he said to Fergus: "Here I have a three-days banquet ready for thee, and I invite thee to come and partake of it."

When Fergus heard this his heart sank and his face waxed all over a crimson red: and he said fiercely to Barach:—"Thou hast done an evil thing to ask me to this banquet: for well thou knowest I cannot refuse thee. Thou knowest, too, that I am under solemn pledge to send the Sons of Usna this very hour to Emain: and if I remain feasting in thy house, how shall I see that my promise of safety is respected?"

But none the less did Barach persist; for he was one of the partners in Concobar's treacherous design.

Then Fergus turned to Naisi and said:—"I dare not violate my knighthood promise: what am I to do in this strait?" But Deirdre answered for her husband:—"The choice is before thee, Fergus; and it is more meet for thee to abandon thy feast than to abandon the sons of Usna, who have come over on thy pledge."

Then Fergus was in sore perplexity; and pondering a little he said:—"I will not forsake the sons of Usna: for I will send with them to Emain Macha my two sons, Illan the Fair and Buinni the Red, who will be their pledge instead of me."

But Naisi said: "We need not thy sons for guard or pledge: we have ever been accustomed to defend ourselves!" And he moved from the place in great wrath:

and his two brothers, and Deirdre, and the two sons of Fergus followed him, with the rest of the clan; while Fergus remained behind silent and[Pg 70]gloomy: for his heart misgave him that mischief was brewing for the sons of Usna.

Then Deirdre tried to persuade the sons of Usna to go to Rathlin between Erin and Alban, and tarry there till Barach's feast was ended: but they did not consent to do so, for they deemed it would be a mark of cowardice: and they sped on by the shortest ways towards Emain Macha.

When now they had come to Fincarn of the Watch-tower on Slieve Fuad, Deirdre and her attendants stayed behind the others a little: and she fell asleep. And when Naisi missed her he turned back and found her just awakening; and he said to her:—"Why didst thou tarry, my princess?"

And she answered:—"I fell asleep and had a dream. And this is what I saw in my dream:—Illan the Fair took your part: Buinni the Red did not: and I saw Illan without his head: but Buinni had neither wound nor hurt."

"Alas, O beauteous princess," said Naisi, "thou utterest nought but evil forebodings: but the king is true and will not break his plighted word."

So they fared on till they had come to the Ridge of the Willows,[25] an hour's journey from the palace: and Deirdre, looking upwards in great fear, said to Naisi:—"O Naisi, see yonder cloud in the sky over Emain, a fearful chilling cloud of a blood-red tinge:[Pg 71]a baleful red cloud that bodes disaster! Come ye now to Dundalgan and abide there with the mighty hero Cuculainn till Fergus returns from Barach's feast; for I fear Concobar's treachery."

But Naisi answered:—"We cannot follow thy advice, beloved Deirdre, for it would be a mark of fear: and we have no fear."

And as they came nigh the palace Deirdre said to them:—"I will now give you a sign if Concobar meditates good or evil. If you are brought into his own mansion where he sits surrounded by his nobles, to eat and drink with him, this is a token that he means no ill; for no man will injure a guest that has partaken of food at his table: but if you are sent to the house of the Red Branch, be sure he is bent on treachery."

When at last they arrived at the palace they knocked loudly with the handwood: and the door-keeper swang the great door wide open. And when he had spoken with them he went and told Concobar that the sons of Usna and Fergus's two sons had come, with their people.

And Concobar called to him his stewards and attendants and asked them:—"How is it in the house of the Red Branch as to food and drink?" And they replied that if the seven battalions of Ulaid were to come to it they would find enough of all good things "If that is so," said Concobar, "take the sons of Usna and their people to the Red Branch."

Even then Deirdre besought them not to enter the Red Branch: for she deemed now that of a certainty there was mischief afoot. But Illan the Fair said:—"Never did we show cowardice or unmanliness, and we shall not do so now." Then she was silent and went with them into the house.

And the company, when they had come in, sat them down so that they filled the great hall: and alluring viands and delicious drinks were set before them: and they ate and drank till they became satisfied and cheerful: all except Deirdre and the Sons of Usna, who did not partake much of food or drink. And Naisi asked for the king's chessboard and chessmen; which were brought: and he and Deirdre began to play.

XIV.

TROUBLE LOOMING.

Let us now speak of Concobar. As he sat among his nobles, the thought of Deirdre came into his mind, and he said:—"Who among you will go to the Red Branch and bring me tidings of Deirdre, whether her youthful shape and looks still live upon her: for if so there is not on the ridge of the world a woman more beautiful." And Lavarcam said she would go.

Now the Sons of Usna were very dear to Lavarcam: and Naisi was dearer than the others. And rising up she went to the Red Branch, where she found Naisi and Deirdre with the chessboard between them, playing. And she saluted them affectionately: and she embraced Deirdre, and wept over her, and kissed her many times with the eagerness of her love: and she kissed the cheeks of Naisi and of his brothers.

And when her loving greeting was ended, she said:—"Beloved children, evil is the deed that is to be done this night in Emain: for the three torches of valour of the Gaels will be treacherously assailed, and Concobar is certainly resolved to put them to death. And now set your people on guard, and bolt and bar all doors, and close all windows; and besteadfast and valourous, and defend your dear chargeman fully, if you may hold the assailants at bay till Fergus comes." And she departed weeping piteously.

And when Lavarcam had returned to Concobar asked what tidings she brought. "Good tidings have I," said she: "for the three Sons of Usna have come, the three valiant champions of Ulaid: and now that they are with thee, O king, thou wilt hold sway in Erin without dispute. And bad tidings I bring also: Deirdre indeed is not as she was, for her youthful form and the splendour of her countenance have fled from her."

And when Concobar heard this his jealousy abated, and he joined in the feasting.

But again the thought of Deirdre came to him, and he asked:—"Who now will go for me to the Red Branch and bring me further tidings of Deirdre and of the Sons of Usna?" for he distrusted Lavarcam. But the Knights of the Red Branch had misgivings of some evil design, and all remained silent.

Then he called to him Trendorn, one of the lesser chiefs: and he said:—"Knowest thou, Trendorn, who slew thy father and thy three brothers in battle?" And Trendorn answered:—"Verily, it was Naisi the son of Usna that slew them." Then the king said:—"Go now to the Red Branch and bring me back tidings of Deirdre and of the Sons of Usna."

Trendorn went right willingly. But when he found the doors and windows of the Red Branch shut up, he was seized with fear, and he said: "It is not safe to approach the Sons of Usna, for they are surely in wrathful mood: nevertheless I must needs bring back tidings to the king."

Whereupon, not daring to knock at the door, he climbed nimbly to a small window high up that had been unwittingly left open, through which he viewed the spacious banquet hall, and saw Naisi and Deirdre playing chess. Deirdre chanced to look up at that moment, and seeing the face of the spy with eyes intently gazing on her, she started with affright[Pg 75]and grasped Naisi's arm, as he was making a move with the chessman. Naisi, following her gaze, and seeing the evil-looking face, flung the chessman withunerring aim and broke the eye in Trendorn's head.

Trendorn dropped down in pain and rage; and going straight to Concobar, he said:—"I have tidings for thee, O king: the three Sons of Usna are sitting in the banquet hall, stately and proud like kings: and Deirdre is seated beside Naisi; and verily, for beauty and queenly grace, her peer cannot be found."

When Concobar heard this, a flame of jealousy and fury blazed up in his heart, and he resolved that by no means should the Sons of Usna escape the doom he planned for them.

XV.

THE ATTACK ON THE SONS OF USNA.

Coming forth on the lawn of Emain, King Concobar now ordered a large body of hireling troops to beset the Red Branch: and he bade them force the doors and bring forth the sons of Usna. And they uttered three dreadful shouts of defiance, and assailed the house on every side; but the strong oak stood bravely, and they were not able to break through doors or walls. So they heaped up great piles of wood and brambles and kindled them till the red flames blazed round the house.

Buinni the Red now stood up and said to the Sons of Usna:—"To me be intrusted the task to repel this first assault: for I am your pledge in place of my father." And marshaling his men, and causing the great door to be thrown wide open, he sallied forth and scattered the assailants and put out the fires: slaying thrice fifty hirelings in that onslaught.

But Buinni returned not to the Red Branch: for the king sent to him with a secret offer of great favours and bribes: namely, his own royal friendship, and a fruitful tract of land; which Buinni took and basely abandoned the sons of Usna. But none the better luck came to him of it: for at that same hour a blight fell on the land, so that it became a moor, waste and profitless, which is at this day called Slieve Fuad.

When Illan the Fair became aware of his brother's treason, he was grieved to the heart, and he said:—"I am the second pledge in place of my father for the sons of Usna, and of a certainty I will not betray them: while this straight sword lives in my hand I will be faithful: and I will now repel this second attack." For at this time the king's hirelings were again thundering at the doors.

Forth he issued with his band: and he made three quick furious circuits round the Red Branch, scattering the troops as he went: after which he returned to the mansion and found Naisi and Deirdre still playing.[26] But as the hireling hordes returned to the attack, he went forth a second time and fell on them, dealing death and havoc whither-soever he went.

Then, while the fight was still raging, Concobar called to him his son Ficra, and said to him:—"Thou and Illan the Fair were born on the same night: and as he has his father's arms, so thou take mine, namely, my shield which is called the Ocean, and my two spears which are called Dart and Slaughter, and my great sword, the Blue-green blade. And bear thyself manfully against him, and vanquish him, else none of my troops will survive."

Ficra did so and went against Illan the Fair; and they made a stout, warlike, red-wounding attack on each other, while the others looked on anxious: but none dared to interfere. And it came to pass that Illan prevailed, so that Ficra was fain to shelter himself behind his father's shield the Ocean, and he was like to be slain. Whereupon the shield moaned, and the Three Waves of Erin uttered their hollow melancholy roar.[27]

The hero Conall Carnagh, sitting in his dun afar off, heard the moan of the shield and the roar of the Wave of Tuath: and springing up from where he sat, he said: "Verily, the king is in danger: I will go to his rescue."

He ran with the swiftness of the wind, and arrived on the Green of Emain where the two young heroes were fighting. Thinking it was Concobar that crouched beneath the shield, he attacked Illan, not knowing him, and wounded him even unto death. And Illan looking up said, "Is it thou, Conall! Alas, dreadful is the deed thou hast done, not knowing me, and not knowing that I am fighting in defence of the Sons of Usna who are now in deadly peril from the treachery of Concobar."

And Conall, finding he had unwittingly wounded his dear young friend Illan, turned in his grief and rage on the other, and swept off his head. And he stalked fierce and silent out of the battlefield.

Illan, still faithful to his charge, called aloud to[Pg 79]Naisi to defend himself bravely: then putting forth his remaining strength, he flung his arms, namely, his sword and his spears and his shield, into the Red Branch; and falling prone on the green sward, the shades of death dimmed his eyes, and his life departed.

And now when it was the dusk of evening, another great battalion of the hirelings assailed the Red Branch, and kindled fagots around it: whereupon Ardan sallied out with his valorous band and scattered them, and put out the fires, and held guard for the first third of the night. And during the second third Ainnli kept them at bay.

Then Naisi took his turn, issuing forth, and fought with them till the morning's dawn: and until the sands of the seashore, or the leaves of the forest, or the dew drops on the grass, or the stars of heaven are counted, it will not be possible to number the hirelings that were slain in that fight by Naisi and his band of heroes.

And as he was returning breathless from the rout, all grimy and terrible with blood and sweat, he spied Lavarcam, as she stood watching the battle anxiously; and he said:—"Go, Lavarcam, go and stand on the outer rampart, and cast thine eyes eastwards, if perchance thou shouldst see Fergus and his men coming."

For many of Naisi's brave followers had fallen in these encounters: and he doubted that he and the others could sustain much longer the continual assaults of superior numbers. And Lavarcam went, but returned downcast, saying she saw nought eastwards, but the open plain with the peaceful herds browsing over it.

XVI.

DEATH OF THE SONS OF USNA.

Believing now that they could no longer defend the Red Branch, Naisi took council with his brothers; and what they resolved on was this:—To sally forth with all their men and fight their way to a place of safety. Then making a close firm fence of shields and spears round Deirdre, they marched out in solid ranks and attacked the hireling battalions and slew three hundred in that onslaught.

Concobar, seeing the rout of his men, and being now sure that it was not possible to subdue the Sons of Usna in open fight, cast about if he might take them by falsehood and craft. And sending for Caffa the druid, who loved them, he said:—

"These sons of Usna are brave men, and it is our pleasure to receive them back into our service. Go now unto them, for thou art their loved friend; and say to them that if they lay down their arms and submit to me, I will restore them to favour and give them[Pg 81]their places among the Red Branch Knights. And I pledge thee my kingly word and my troth as a true knight, that no harm shall befal them."

Caffa, by no means distrusting him, went to the Sons of Usna and told them all the king had said. And they, suspecting neither guile nor treachery joyfully threw their swords and spears aside, and went towards the king to make submission. But now, while they stood defenceless, the king caused them to be seized and bound. Then, turning aside he sought for someone to put them to death; but he found no man of the Ultonians willing to do so.

Among his followers was a foreigner named Maini of the Rough Hand, whose father and two brothers had fallen in battle by Naisi: and this man undertook to kill the Sons of Usna.

When they were brought forth to their doom, Ardan said:—"I am the youngest: let me be slain first that I may not see the death of my brothers." And Ainnli

54

earnestly pleaded for the same thing for himself, saying that he was born before Ardan and should die before him.

But Naisi said:—"Lo, I have a sword, the gift ofMannanan Mac Lir, which leaves no remnant unfinished after a blow: let us be struck with it, all three together, and we shall die at the same moment."

This was agreed to: and the sword was brought forth, and they laid their heads close together, and Maini swept off all three with one blow of the mighty[Pg 82]sword. And when it became known that the Sons of Usna were dead, the men of Ulaid sent forth three great cries of grief and lamentation.

As for Deirdre, she cried aloud, and tore her golden hair, and became like one distracted. And after a time, when her calmness had a little returned, she uttered a lament:—

I.

"Three lions of the hill are dead, and I am left alone to weep for them. The generous princes who made the stranger welcome have been guilefully lured to their doom.

II.

"The three strong hawks of Slieve Cullinn,[28] a king's three sons, strong and gentle: willing obedience was yielded to them by heroes who had conquered many lands.

III.

"Three generous heroes of the Red Branch, who loved to praise the valour of others: three props of the battalions of Quelna: their fall is the cause of bitter grief.

IV.

"Ainnli and Ardan, haughty and fierce in battle, to me were ever loving and gentle: Naisi, Naisi, beloved spouse of my choice, thou canst not hear thy Deirdre lamenting thee.

V.

"When they brought down the fleet red deer in the chase, when they speared the salmon skilfully in the clear water, joyful and proud were they if I looked on.

VI.

55

"Often when my feeble feet grew weary wandering along the valleys, and climbing the hills to view the chase, often would they bear me home lightly on their linked shields and spears.

VII.

"It was gladness of heart to be with the Sons of Usna: long and weary is the day without their company: short will be my span of life since they have left me.

VIII.

"Sorrow and tears have dimmed my eyes, looking at the grave of Naisi: a dark deadly sickness has seized my heart: I cannot, I cannot live after Naisi.

IX.

"O, thou who diggest the new grave, make it deep and wide: let it be a grave for four: for I will sleep for ever beside my beloved."

When she had spoken these words, she fell beside the body of Naisi and died immediately. And a great[Pg 84]cairn of stones was piled over their grave, and their names were inscribed in Ogham, and their funeral rites were performed.

This is the sorrowful tale of The Fate of the Sons of Usna.

XVII.

AVENGING AND BRIGHT.

Avenging and bright fall the swift sword of Erin,On him, who the brave sons of Usna betray'd! For ev'ry fond eye he hath waken'd a tear in, A drop from his heart-wounds shall weep o'er her blade.

By the red cloud that hung over Connor's dark dwelling, When Ulad's three champions lay sleeping in gore—By the billows of war which, so often high swelling,Have wafted these heroes to victory's shore?

We swear to revenge them!—no joy shall be tasted, The harp shall be silent, the maiden unwed, Our halls shall be mute, and our fields shall lie wasted, Till vengeance is wreak'd on the murderer's head.

Yes, monarch! though sweet are our home recollections, Though sweet are the tears that from tenderness fall; Though sweet are our friendships, our hopes, our affections, Revenge[29] on a tyrant is sweetest of all!

Thomas Moore.

XVIII.

THE WRATH OF FERGUS MAC ROY.

Barach's banquet was ended. Fergus, anxious and impatient, returned with his people to Emain. And when he found that the sons of Usna had been slain in violation of his pledge, and that his son, Illan the Fair, had fallen while defending them, his grief and wrath knew no bounds. Caffa the druid was none the less incensed; and he was in sore anguish: for he it was, who, trusting in Concobar's deceitful promises, persuaded the sons of Usna to give up their arms and yield. And he pronounced the doom of Concobar's race, that neither he nor any of his descendants should reign in Emain thenceforward for evermore.

And these two, Fergus and Caffa, collecting their men of valour, spoiled and laid waste Concobar's territory; till at last a battle was fought between them, in which the king was defeated, and three hundred of his bravest Ultonians were slain, besides his son and many other illustrious persons in his service. Fergus and Caffa then attacked Emain, and burned and pillaged it, and slew those who defended it. And though the palace was rebuilt in due time, and continued to be the residence of the kings of Ulaid for more than three hundred years afterwards, none of Concobar's descendants possessed it, as Caffa had foretold.

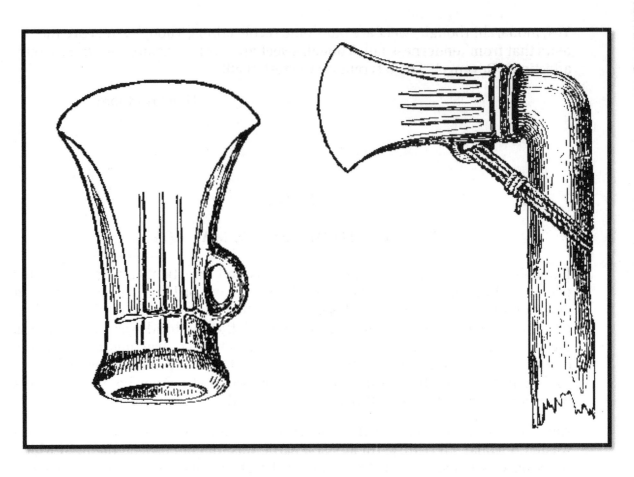

Bronze celts. A celt was a sort of battle axe; sometimes made of bronze, sometimes of stone. The right hand figure shows how the bronze head was fixed to the handle. Great numbers of these celts of many different shapes, both stone and bronze, are preserved in the National Museum, Dublin.

After this, Fergus and other great champions of the Red Branch, with three thousand warriors, marched[Pg 87]into Connaught, where Ailell and Maive, king and queen of that province, being at war with Concobar, welcomed them and took them gladly into their service. And for seven years they continued to send marauding parties to spoil and ravage the province of Ulaid, so that many battles were fought, and many heroes were slain. In the stories of this war we read much of the mighty champion Cuculainn who was the chief defender of Ulaid against Ailell and Maive's forces.

XIX.

ANCIENT IRISH PHYSICIANS: Part I.

Among most nations of old times there were great leeches or physicians, who were considered so skillful that the people believed they could cure wounds and ailments as if by magic. In some countries they became gods, as among the Greeks.

The ancient Irish people, too, had their mighty leech, a Dedannan named Dianket, who, as they believed, could heal all wounds and cure all diseases; so that he became the Irish God of Medicine. He had a son, Midac, and a daughter, Armedda, who were both as good as himself; and at last Midac became so skilful that his father killed him in a fit of jealousy. And, after some time, there grew up[Pg 88]from the young doctor's grave 365 herbs, each with virtue to cure some particular ailment. His sister Armedda plucked up these herbs, and carefully sorting them, wrapped them up in her mantle. But the jealous old Dianket came and mixed them all up, so that no one could distinguish them: and but for this—according to the legend—every physician would now be able to cure all diseases without delay, by selecting and applying the proper herbs.

Leaving these shadowy old-world stories, let us come down to historic times, when we shall, as it were, tread on solid ground. From the very earliest times medicine and surgery were carefully studied in Ireland: and there was a distinct class of professional medical doctors, who underwent a course of education and practical training. A young man usually learned to be a physician by apprenticeship, i.e. by living in the house of a regular physician, and accompanying him on his visits to patients to learn his methods of treatment.

A king or a great chief had always a physician as part of his household, to attend to the health of his family. The usual remuneration of these men was a residence and a tract of land in the neighborhood, free of all rent and taxes, together with certain allowances: and the medical man might, if he chose, practise for fee outside the household. Some of those in the service of great kings had castles, and lived in state like princes. Those not so attached lived on[Pg 89]their fees, like many doctors of the present day: and the fees for the various operations or attendances were laid down in the Brehon Law.[30]

Though medical doctors were looked up to with great respect, they had to be very careful in exercising their profession. A leech who through carelessness, or willful neglect, or gross want of skill, failed to cure a wound, might be brought before a brehon or judge, and if the case was proved home against him, he had to pay the same fine to the patient, as if he had inflicted the wound with his own hand.

59

XX.

ANCIENT IRISH PHYSICIANS: Part II.

Medicine, as a profession, like Law, History, &c., often ran in families in Ireland, descending regularly from father to son; and several Irish families were distinguished leeches for generations, such as the O'Shiels, the O'Cassidys, the O'Hickeys, and the O'Lees.

Each medical family kept a book, which was handed down reverently from father to son, and in which was written, in Irish or Latin, all the medical knowledge derived either from other books or from the actual experience of the various members[Pg 90]of the family; and many of these old volumes, all in beautiful handwriting, are still preserved in Dublin and elsewhere. As showing the admirable spirit in which those good men studied and practised their profession, and how much they loved it, it is worthwhile to give a translation of the opening statement, a sort of preface, in the Irish language, written at the beginning of one of these books, in the year 1352.

"May the good God have mercy on us all. I have here collected practical rules of medicine from several works, for the honour of God, for the benefit of the Irish people, for the instruction of my pupils, and for the love of my friends and of my kindred. I have translated many of them into Gaelic from Latin books, containing the lore of the great leeches of Greece and Rome. These are sweet and profitable things which have been often tested by us and by our instructors.

"I pray God to bless those doctors who will use this book; and I lay it as an injunction on their souls, that they extract knowledge from it not by any means sparingly, and that they do not neglect the practical rules herein contained. More especially I charge them that they do their duty devotedly in cases where they receive no payment on account of the poverty of their patients.

"Let every physician, before he begins his treatment, offer up a secret prayer for the sick person, and implore the heavenly Father, the Physician and[Pg 91]Balm-giver of all mankind, to prosper the work he is entering upon, and to save himself and his patient from failure."

There is good reason to believe that the noble sentiments here expressed were generally those of the physicians of the time; from which we may see that the old Irish medical doctors were quite as devoted to their profession, as eager for knowledge, and as anxious about their patients as those of the present day.

The fame of the Irish physicians reached the continent. Even at a comparatively late time, about three hundred years ago, when medicine had been successfully studied and practised in Ireland for more than a thousand years, a well-known and distinguished physician of Brussels,[31] in a book written by him in Latin on medical subjects, praises the Irish doctors, and describes them correctly as follows:—

"In the household of every great lord in Ireland there is a physician who has a tract of land for his support, and who is appointed to his post, not on account of the great amount of learning he brings away in his head from colleges, but because he is able to cure diseases. His knowledge of the healing art is derived from books left him by his forefathers, which describe very exactly the marks and signs by which the various diseases are known, and lay down[Pg 92]the proper remedies for each. These remedies, [which are mostly herbs], are all produced in that country. Accordingly, the Irish people are much better managed in sickness than the Italians, who have a physician in every village."

It is pleasant to know that the Irish physicians of our time who, it is generally agreed, are equal to those of any other country in the world, can look back with respect, and not without some feeling of pride, to their Irish predecessors of the times of old.

XXI.

THE FENA OF ERIN.

In the third century of the Christian era lived the Fena[32] of Erin, a famous body of warriors something like the Red Branch Knights of an older time. Their most renowned commander was Finn Mac Cumaill [Cool], King Cormac Mac Art's son-in-law, who of all the heroes of ancient Ireland is at the present day best remembered in tradition by the people.

Finn had his chief residence on the Hill of Allen, a remarkable flat-topped hill lying about four miles to the right of the railway as you pass from Newbridge towards Kildare, which will be at once recognised by a tall pillar erected fifty or sixty years ago on[Pg 93]the top, on the very site of Finn's palace. There are now very little remains of the palace-fort, which, there is good reason to believe, was at no time very large. Whatever remained of it has been cleared away, partly to make room for the pillar, and partly by cultivation, for the land has been tilled and cropped to the very summit. The whole neighbourhood however still teems with living traditions of the heroes; and the people all round the hill tell many stories of Finn and the Fena, and point out the several spots they frequented. As in the case of the Red Branch Knights, there were Fena in all the provinces, each provincial troop under a leader. The Fena of Erin flourished for many generations; but they reached their greatest glory under Finn in the time of Cormac Mac Art, who was king of Ireland from A.D. 254 to 277.

No man was admitted to their ranks till he had proved his strength and activity by passing severe tests in leaping, running, and defending himself from attack against great odds. They should be educated in the sort of learning in vogue at the time, and especially they should be able to repeat many verses and stories recounting the great deeds of the times of old, so that they might learn to admire all that was brave and noble, and that in time of peace they might be bright and entertaining at banquets and other festive gatherings. They were all mighty men in fight, brave, and strong, and swift of foot: and[Pg 94]they were above all things bound to be honourable and truthful in their dealings, and to protect the weak—particularly women and children—from oppression and wrong.

The Fena loved open-air games and exercises of all kinds, especially the chase. They had a breed of enormous dogs of which they were very fond, gentle and affectionate at home, but fierce and terrible in the chase; and from Beltane (1st of May) to Samin (1st November) they hunted deer, wild boars, and other game through the forests, and over the hills, glens, and plains. Though the chief men among them rode on horseback when travelling long distances from one district to another, they always hunted on foot, never using horses in the chase. During hunting time they camped out at night, living on the flesh of the animals they brought down and on the wild fruit and herbs of the forest.

At midday, whatever game they had killed during the morning they sent by their attendants to the place appointed for the evening meal, which was always chosen near a wood and beside a stream or lake. The attendants roasted one part on hazel spits before immense fires of wood, and baked the rest on hot stones in a pit dug in the earth. The stones were heated in the fires. At the bottom of the pit the men placed a layer of these hot stones: then a layer of meat-joints wrapped in sedge to keep them from being burned: next another layer of hot stones:[Pg 95]down on that more meat; and so on till the whole was disposed of. When the hunters returned, their first care was to bathe, so as to remove the sweat and mire of the chase. Then they attended to their hair: for they wore the hair long, and were very particular about combing, dressing, and plaiting it. By the time their preparations were completed, the meat was ready: and the hungry hunters sat down to their smoking-hot savoury meal.

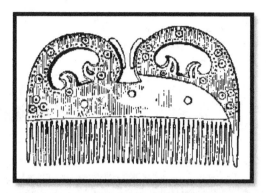
Ancient Irish ornamented comb in the National Museum, Dublin.

Ancient Irish gold earring, one of a pair found in Co. Roscommon

After the meal they set up their tents, and each man prepared his bed. He first put down a thick layer of brushwood from the surrounding forest; on that he spread a quantity of moss; and on that again a layer of fresh rushes, on which he slept soundly after his day of joyous, healthful toil. In the old tales these three materials—brushwood, moss, and rushes—are called the "Three beddings of the Fena."[33]

The Fena were in the service of the kings, and their main duties were to uphold justice and put down oppression and wrong, to suppress robbers and other evil-doers, to exact fines and tributes for the king, and to guard the harbours of the country against pirates and invaders. For these services they received a fixed pay: during the six months hunting season, their pay was merely the animals they killed, of which they used the flesh for food and sold the skins.

An Irish poet of our day has written of the Milesian people in general, including those Fena of Erin and the Red Branch Knights:—

"Long, long ago, beyond the misty space Of twice a thousand years, In Erin old there dwelt a mighty race Taller than Roman spears; Like oaks and towers they had a giant grace, Were fleet as deers, With winds and wave they made their biding place, Those western shepherd seers.

Great were their deeds, their passions, and their sports. With clay and stone, They piled on strath and shore those mystic forts, Not yet o'erthrown: On cairn-crowned hills they held their council-courts; While youths alone, With giant dogs explored the elk resorts And brought them down."

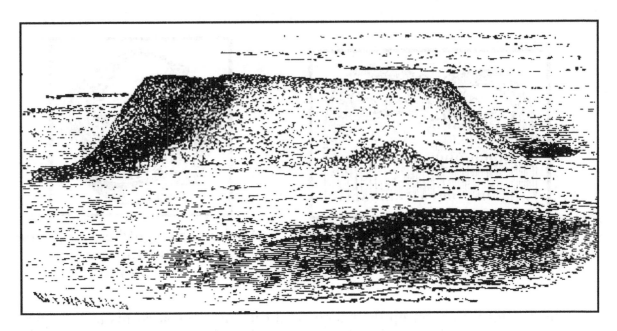

Cairn, on Carns Hill near Sligo: a "cairn-crowned hill."

In many modern stories, Finn is spoken of as a giant; but this is a vulgar notion. The old romantic tales describe him as a tall, strong man, though not a giant; with much keen wit, sound sense, and great judgment: and though he was a mighty champion, he ruled his men more by wisdom, kindness, and justice, than by strength. When quite a young man his hair became white like silver: how this happened will be told in the next story. Oisin [Isheen] or Ossian, the renowned hero-poet of the Fena, was his son. Oscar the son of Ossian was youthful, comely, kind-hearted, and valiant. Dermot O'Dyna was the handsomest of all these heroes. He was unconquerably brave, of untarnished honour, generous, and self-denying, ever ready to take the post of danger, always giving credit to others, and never in the least boasting of his own deeds. He is the finest character of all the Fena; and it would be hard to find his[Pg 98]equal in the ancient tales of any country. We have a vast number of beautiful stories in the Irish language about Finn and the other heroes of the Fena, a few of which are translated in this book.

XXII.

THE CHASE OF SLIEVE CULLINN.

64

IN WHICH OSSIAN RELATES HOW FINN'S HAIR WAS CHANGED IN ONE DAY FROM THE COLOUR OF GOLD TO SILVERY GREY.

On a morning in summer, Finn happened to be walking alone on the lawn before the palace of Allen, when a doe sprang out from a thicket, and, passing quite close to him, bounded past like the wind. Without a moment's delay, he signalled for his companions and dogs; but none heard except his two hounds, Bran and Skolan. He instantly gave chase, accompanied only by his two dogs; and before the Fena knew of his absence, he had left Allen of the green slopes far behind.

The chase turned northwards; and though the hounds kept close to the doe, the chief kept quite as close to the hounds the whole way. And so they continued without rest or pause, till they reached Slieve Cullinn, far in the north.

Here the doe made a sudden turn and disappeared; and Finn never caught sight of her after. And he marvelled much that any doe in the world should be able to lead Bran and Skolan so long a chase, and escape from them in the end. Meantime they kept searching, Finn taking one side of the hill and the dogs another, so that he was at last left quite alone.

While he was wandering about the hill and whistling for his hounds, he heard the plaintive cry of a woman at no great distance; and, turning his steps towards the place, he saw a beautiful young lady sitting on the brink of a little lake, weeping as if her heart would break. Finn accosted her; and, seeing that she ceased her weeping for a moment, he asked her had she seen his two hounds pass that way.

"I have not seen thy hounds," she replied, "nor have I been at all concerned in the chase; for, alas, there is something that troubles me more nearly. I had a precious gold bracelet on my hand, which I prized beyond anything in the world; and it has fallen from me into the water. I saw it roll down the steep slope at the bottom, till it went quite out of my sight. This is the cause of my sorrow, and thou canst remedy the mishap if thou wilt. The Fena are sworn never to refuse help to a woman in distress; and I now put it on thee to search for this bracelet, and cease not till thou find it and restore it to me."

Finn plunged in without a moment's hesitation;[Pg 100]and after swimming three times round the lake, diving and searching into every nook and cranny at the bottom, he found the bracelet at last; and approaching the lady, he handed it to her from the water. The moment she had got it she sprang into the lake before his eyes, and, diving down, disappeared in an instant.

65

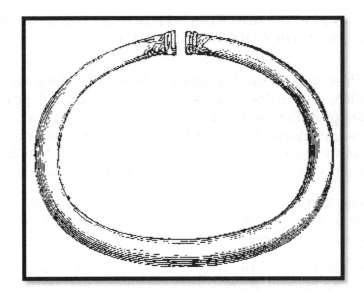

Irish bracelet or armlet of solid gold, now in the National Museum, Dublin. It is double the size of the picture, of beautiful shape and workmanship, and weighs 3¾ oz.

The chief, wondering greatly at this strange behaviour, stepped forth from the water; but as soon as his feet had touched the dry land, he lost all his strength, and fell on the brink, a withered, grey old man, shrunken up and trembling all over with weakness. He sat him down in woful plight; and soon his hounds came up. They looked at him wistfully and sniffed and whined around him; but they knew him not, and, passing on, they ran round the lake, searching in vain for their master.

On that day we and the Fena in general were assembled in the banquet hall of the palace of Allen; some feasting, some playing chess, and others listening to the sweet music of the harpers. While all were in this wise pleasantly engaged, we suddenly missed our chief, and when we searched for him he was nowhere to be found: whereupon we became alarmed. Inquiring now from the lesser people about the palace, we found that the chief and his two dogs had chased a doe northwards. So, having mustered a strong party of the Fena, we started in pursuit, and following the track, never slackened speed till we reached Slieve Cullinn.

We began to search round the hill, and after wandering among brakes and rough, rocky places, we at last espied a grey-headed old man sitting on the brink of a lake. I went up to him, followed by the rest of the Fena, and asked him if he had seen a noble-looking hero pass that way, with two hounds, chasing a doe. He never answered a word, neither did he stir from where he sat, or even look up; but at the question, his head sank on his breast, and his limbs shook all over as with palsy. Then he fell into a sudden fit of grief, wringing his hands and uttering feeble cries of woe.

We soothed him and used him gently, hoping he might speak at last; but to no purpose, for he only lamented the more, and still answered nothing.

At last, after this had gone on for some time, and[Pg 102]when we were about to leave him, he told us in a whisper the dreadful secret; and then we all came to know the truth. When we found that the withered old man was no other than our beloved king, Finn himself, we uttered three shouts of lamentation and anger, so loud and prolonged that the foxes and badgers rushed affrighted from their dens in the hollows of the mountain.

When quietness was restored, we asked Finn how this dread evil had befallen him; and he told us that it was the daughter of Culann the smith who had transformed him by her spells. And then he recounted how she had lured him to swim in the lake, and how, when he came forth, he was turned into a withered old man.

We now made a framework litter of slender poles, and, placing our king on it, we lifted him tenderly on our shoulders. And, turning from the lake, we marched slowly up-hill till we came to the fairy palace of Slieve Cullinn, where we knew the daughter of Culann had her dwelling deep underground. Here we set him down, and the whole troop began at once to dig, determined to find the enchantress in her cave-palace, and force her to restore our chief.

For three days and three nights we dug, without a moment's rest or pause, till at length we reached her hollow dwelling; when she, affrighted at the tumultand at the vengeful look of the heroes, suddenly started forth from the cave and stood before us. She held in her hand a drinking-horn of red gold, which she handed to the king and told him to drink. No sooner had he drunk from it, than his own shape and features returned, save only that his hair remained of a silvery grey.

When we gazed on our chief in his own graceful and manly form, we were all pleased with the soft, silvery hue of the grey hairs. And, though the enchantress appeared ready to restore this also, Finn himself told her that it pleased him as it pleased the others, and that he chose to remain grey for the rest of his life.

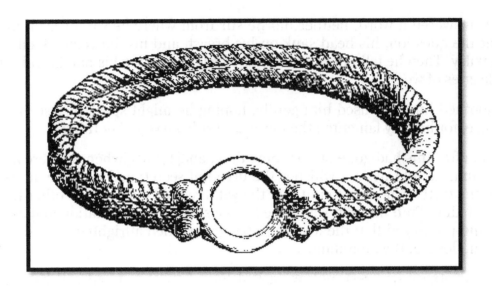

Ancient Irish bracelet for the wrist. This is of bronze; but many Irish bracelets were of gold

---

XXIII.

SAINT BRIGIT: PART I.

Of all the Irish saints, Brigit and Columkille are, next after St. Patrick, the most loved and revered by the people of Ireland.

Like many others of our early saints, Brigit came of a noble family. Her father Dubthach [Duffa] was a distinguished Leinster chief, descended from the kings of Ireland. For some reason, which we do not know, he and his wife lived for a time in Faughart near Dundalk, which was then a part of Ulster: and at Faughart Brigit was born about the year 455. The family must have soon returned however to their own district, for we know that Brigit passed her childhood with her parents in the neighbourhood of Kildare. She was baptised, and carefully instructed and trained, both in general education and in religion: for her father and mother were Christians. As she grew up, her quiet, gentle, modest ways pleased all that knew her. At the time of her birth, St. Patrick was in the midst of his glorious career; and some say that while she was still a child she knew him, and that when he died she made with her own hands a winding sheet in which his body was laid in the grave; which may have happened, as she was ten or twelve years of age at the time of his death.

When Brigit came of an age to choose her way of life, she resolved to be a nun, to which her parents made no objection. After due preparation she went to a holy bishop of the neighbourhood, who, at her request, received her, and placed a white robe on her shoulders and a white veil over her head. Here she remained for some time in companionship with eight[Pg 105]other maidens who had been received with her, and who placed themselves under her guidance. As time went on, she became so beloved for her piety and sweetness of disposition, that many young women asked to be admitted; so that though she by no means desired that people should be speaking in her praise, the fame of her little community began to spread through the country.

This first establishment was conducted strictly under a set of Rules drawn up by Brigit herself: and now, bishops in various parts of Ireland began to apply to her to establish convents in their several districts under the same rules. She was glad of this, and she did what she could to meet their wishes. She visited Longford, Tipperary, Limerick, South Leinster, and Roscommon, one after another; and in all these places she founded convents.

At last the people of her own province of Leinster, considering that they had the best right to her services, sent a number of leading persons to request that she would fix her permanent residence among them. She was probably pleased to go back to live in the place where she had spent her childhood; and she returned to Leinster, where she was welcomed with great joy. The Leinster people gave her a piece of land chosen by herself, on the edge of a beautiful level grassy plain, well known as the Curragh of Kildare. Here, on a low ridge over-looking the plain, she built a little church, under the[Pg 106]shade of a wide-spreading oak tree, whence it got the name of Kill-dara, the Church of the Oak, or as we now call it, Kildare. This tree continued to flourish long after Brigit's death, and it was regarded with great veneration by the people of the place. A writer of the tenth century—four hundred years after the foundation of the church—tells us that in his time it was a mere branchless, withered trunk; but the people had such reverence for it that no one dared to cut or chip it.

We are not quite sure of the exact year of Brigit's settlement here; but it probably occurred about 485, when she was thirty years of age. Hard by the church she also built a dwelling for herself and her community. We are told, in the Irish Life of St. Brigit, that this first house was built of wood, like the houses of the people in general: and the little church under the oak was probably of wood also, like most churches of the time. As the number of applicants for admission continued to increase, both church and dwelling had to be enlarged from time to time; and the wood was replaced by stone and mortar. Such was the respect in which the good abbess was held, that visitors came from all parts of the country to see her and ask her advice and blessing: and many of them settled down in the place, so that a town gradually grew up near the convent, which was the beginning of the town of Kildare.

XXIV.

SAINT BRIGIT: PART II.

Brigit, although now at the head of a great community, and very strict in carrying out her Rules, still retained all her humility and gentleness of disposition. With such a large family, there was plenty of work to do; and it was all done by the nuns, as they kept no servants and called in no outsiders. The abbess herself, so far as she was able to withdraw from the cares of governing the establishment, took her part like the rest in most of the domestic occupations. In some of the old accounts of her life we are told that she often, with some companions, herded and tended her flocks of sheep that grazed on the level sward round the convent. And sometimes she was caught by the heavy rain-squalls that occasionally sweep across that shelterless plain, so that her clothes were wet through by the time she returned to the convent: showing that she took her own share of the rough work.

Not far from the convent, another establishment was founded, later on, for men, which afterwards became one of the great Colleges of Ireland. As the two communities and the population of the town continued to grow, it was Brigit's earnest desire that a bishop should be there to take spiritual charge of the whole place. A holy man named Conleth, who had hitherto spent his life as a hermit in the neighbourhood, was appointed bishop by the heads of the Church. He was the first bishop of Kildare, and he took up his residence in the monastery. The name of that good bishop is to this day held in affectionate remembrance, with that of St. Brigit, by the people of Kildare and of the country all round.

Ruins of Kilcrea Abbey, on the river Bride, ten miles from Cork city. Built in honour of St. Brigit.

While the parent convent at Kildare continued to grow, branch houses under Brigit's Rule, and subject to her authority, were established all over Ireland; and many establishments for monks were also founded in honour of her.

Brigit had such a reputation for wisdom and prudence, that the most eminent of the saints, and many kings and chiefs of her day, visited Kildare or corresponded with her, to obtain her advice in doubtful or difficult matters. Visitors were constantly coming and going, all of whom she received kindly and treated hospitably. All this, with daily alms to the needy, and the support of a large community, kept her poor: for the produce of her land was not nearly sufficient to supply her wants. For a long time in the beginning she and her community suffered from downright poverty, so that she had often to call on the charity of her friends and neighbours to assist her. But as time went on, and as the reputation of the place spread abroad, she received many presents from rich people, which generally came in the right time, and enabled her to carry on her establishment without any danger of want.

Among Brigit's virtues none is more marked than her charity and kindness of heart towards poor, needy, and helpless people. She never could look on distress of any kind without trying to relieve it at whatever cost. Even when a mere girl living with her parents, her father was often displeased with her for giving away necessary things belonging to the house to poor people who came in their[Pg 110]misery to beg from her. It happened on one occasion that her father drove her in his chariot to Naas (in Kildare), where then lived Dunlang king of Leinster; and dismounting, he entered the palace, leaving his sword behind—a beautiful and valuable one—while Brigit remained in charge of horse and chariot. A wretched looking poor man with sickness and want in his face came up and begged for some relief. Overcome with pity she looked about for something to give him, and finding nothing but the sword, she handed it to him. On her father's return he fell into a passion at the loss of his sword: and when King Dunlang questioned her reproachfully, she replied:—"If I had all thy wealth I would give it to the poor; for giving to the poor is giving to the Lord of the Universe." And the king turning to the father said:—"It is not meet that either you or I should chide this maiden, for her merit is greater before God than before men": on which the matter ended: and Brigit returned home with her father.

Her overflowing kindness of heart was not confined to human beings: it extended even to the lower animals. Once while she lived in her father's house, a party of guests were invited, and she was given some pieces of meat to cook for dinner. And a poor miserable half-starved hound limped into the house and looked longingly at the meat: whereupon the girl, quite unable to overcome her feeling of pity, threw him one of the pieces.[Pg 111]And when the poor animal, in his hungry greediness, had devoured that in a moment, she gave him another, which satisfied him. And to the last day of her life she retained her tenderness of heart and her kindness and charity towards the poor.

XXV.

SAINT BRIGIT: PART III.

Late in life Brigit's influence over young people was unbounded: for her very gentleness gave tenfold power to her words. Once, seeing a young man, a student of the neighbouring college, running very violently and in an unbecoming manner, in presence of some of her nuns, she sent for him on the spot and asked him why he was running in such haste. He replied thoughtlessly, and half in jest, that he was running to heaven: on which she said quietly: "I wish to God, my dear son, that I was worthy to run with you to-day to the same place: I beg you will pray for me to help me to arrive there." And when he heard these words, and looked on her gravekind face, he was greatly moved; and telling her with tears in his eyes, that he would surely pray for her and for many others besides, he besought her to offer up her prayers for him, that he might continue his journey steadily towards heaven, and arrive there[Pg 112]in the end. That young man, whose name was Ninnius, became in after-life one of the most revered of the Irish saints.

But with all her gentle unassuming ways, St. Brigit was a woman of strong mind and greattalents. She not only governed her various establishments in strict accordance with her own Rules and forms of discipline, but she was a powerful aid in forwarding the mighty religious movement that had been commenced by St. Patrick half a century before. She set an illustrious example to those Irish women who, during and after her time, entered on a religious life; and though many of them became distinguished saints, she stands far above them all. No writer has left us a detailed account of her last hours, as Adamnan has done for St. Columkille. (See page 150, note, farther on.) We only know that she died at Kildare on the first of February, in or about the year 523, and that she received the last consolations of religion from the grateful hand of that same Ninnius whom she had turned to a religious life many years before.

She was buried in Kildare, where her body was entombed in a magnificent shrine, ornamented with gold, silver, and precious stones. We may be sure it was a very beautiful work of art, for we know that there was a noted school of metal workers in Kildare under the direction of St. Conleth, who was himself a most skilful artist; but this tomb was plundered[Pg 113]by the Danes three hundred years afterwards, and not a trace of it now remains.

According to some accounts, the bones of St. Brigit and St. Columkille were brought to Downpatrick many centuries after the death of both, and buried in the same tomb with the remains of St. Patrick. Whether this was so or not, the matter has been commemorated in a Latin verse, of which the following is a translation:—

"Interred beneath one tomb in Down, a single vault doth holdPatrick and Brigit and Columkille, three holy saints of old."

A well known Welshman, Gerald Barry (Giraldus Cambrensis), who was in Ireland in 1185, and who wrote an account of it, says that he found "at Kildare in Leinster, celebrated for the glorious Brigit, the 'Fire of St. Brigit' which is reported never to go out." This fire was kept up day and night by the nuns in his time, and for centuries before—how long no one can tell—probably from the time of the saint herself—and was continued for centuries after: but it was finally extinguished when the monasteries were closed up by Henry VIII. in the year 1536. Thomas Moore, in one of his songs, refers to it in the following words:—

"Like the bright lamp that shone in Kildare's holy fane,And burned through long ages of darkness and storm."

St. Brigit is venerated in England and Scotland as well as in Ireland: for in both these countries churches were built in her honour, and many convents were established under her name and rule. She was also well known and honoured on the Continent. We need not wonder that her life has been written by many Irishmen: but English, Scotch, French, Italian, and German writers have also written about her and have commemorated her as one of the most eminent saints of the West.

Convents and monasteries were maintained in Kildare for hundreds of years after the time of St. Brigit; and "Kildare's holy fane" is still venerated as much as ever. On the very ridge where the humble little church was erected fourteen hundred years ago, there is a group of fine old church buildings, with a tall round tower that overlooks the splendid plain of Kildare.

XXVI.

IRISH SCRIBES AND BOOKS.

In old times all books were handwritten, printing being a late invention. There were persons called Scribes, many of whom made writing the chief business of their lives. From constant practice they[Pg 115]became very expert; and the penmanship of many of them was extremely beautiful and highly ornamented, much more so than any writing executed by the very best penmen of the present day.

In Ireland, most of these scribes were monks, inmates of monasteries; but many were laymen. These good and industrious men wrote into their books all the learning of every kind that they could collect; so that although the work of writing was slow, the numbers of books rapidly increased; and very large libraries grew up, especially in the monasteries. The leaves of these books were not paper like those of our books, but parchment or vellum, which was generally made from sheepskin, but often from the skins of other animals.

Sometimes the scribes wrote down what had never been written before, that is, matters composed at the time, or preserved in memory: but more commonly they copied from other volumes. If an old book began to be worn, ragged, or dim with age, so as to be hard to make out and read, some scribe was sure to copy it, so as to have a new book easy to read and well bound up. Most of the books written out in this manner related to Ireland, as will be described presently; and the language of these was almost always Irish. For in those times the Irish language was spoken by all the people of Ireland.

A favourite occupation was copying portions of the Holy Scriptures, nearly always in the Latin language;[Pg 116]and in this good work some monks spent nearly all their time, in order to multiply copies of the sacred books. Some of the greatest saints of the ancient Irish Church employed themselves in copying the Gospels and other portions of the Bible, whenever they could get the opportunity, as we shall see in the case of St. Columkille.

Copies of the Scriptures, and also prayer books, were generally ornamented in the most beautiful way: for those accomplished and devoted old scribes loved to beautify the sacred writings. Many of the lovely books they wrote are still preserved, of which the most splendid is the Book of Kells, now kept in the Library of Trinity College, in Dublin. It is a copy of the Four Gospels, and the language is Latin, though the letters are Irish. It was written by an Irish scribe eleven or twelve hundred years ago, but who he was is not known.

There is no old book in any part of the world so skillfully ornamented as this. The capital letters are very large—one of them fills an entire page—and are all illuminated, that is, painted in brilliant colours; and after the lapse of so many centuries the colours are still very fresh, though not so bright as when they were first laid on.

In this Book of Kells, and in others like it, the capitals are ornamented in every part with a kind of interlaced work, all done with the pen, in which bands and ribbons are curved and plaited and[Pg 117]woven in the most wonderful way. These plaits and folds are so small and so close together that one must sometimes use a magnifying glass in order to see them plainly: in one space, the size of a half penny, in a page of a splendid old volume, called the Book of Armagh, the ribbons appear woven in and out more than three hundred times.

A specimen of this interwoven ornamental work is seen at the head of the first page of this book; but it gives only a poor idea of the beauty of the Book of Kells. The frontispiece of the "Child's History of Ireland" is a perfect copy, in full colours, of a complete page of the Book of Mac Durnan, which is almost as beautiful as the Book of Kells. The Irish used this sort of ornamentation also in metal-work and stone-work, of which an example is given here.

Ancient Irish Ornamental Sculpture on a Stone Monument.

Very often, large volumes were kept, into which were written compositions of all kinds, both prose and poetry, such as were thought worth preserving, copied from older books, and written in, one after[Pg 118]another, till the volume was filled. Of all these old books of mixed compositions, the largest that remains to us is the Book of Leinster, which is kept in Trinity College in Dublin. It is an immense volume, all in the Irish language, written more than 750 years ago; and many of the pages are now almost black with age and very hard to make out. It contains a great number of pieces, some in prose and some in verse, and nearly all of them about Ireland—histories, accounts of battles and sieges, lives and adventures of great men, with many tales and stories of things that happened in this country in far distant ages.

The Book of the Dun Cow is preserved in the Royal Irish Academy in Dublin. It is fifty years older than the Book of Leinster, but not so large; and it contains also a great number of tales, adventures, and histories, nearly all relating to Ireland, and all written in the Irish language. Its name was derived from the following circumstance:—St. Kieranof Clonmacnoise had a favourite brown cow, whose skin, when she died, he caused to be turned into parchment, of which a book was made. But this old book no longer exists: it was lost ages ago; and the present "Book of the Dun Cow" is only a copy of it.

Three other great Irish books kept in Dublin are the Book of Lecan [Leckan], the Yellow Book of Lecan, and the Book of Ballymote. These contain[Pg 119]much the same kind of matter as the Book of Leinster—with pieces mostly different however—but they are not nearly so old. The Speckled Book, which is also in Dublin, is nearly as large as the Book of Leinster, but not so old. It is mostly on religious matters, and contains a great number of Lives of Saints, Hymns,

Sermons, portions of the Scriptures, and other such pieces. All these books are written with the greatest care, and in most beautiful penmanship.

The six old books described above have been lately printed, in such a way as that the print resembles exactly the writing of the old books themselves. The printed volumes are now to be found in libraries in several parts of Ireland, as well as in England and the Continent; so that those desirous of studying them need not come to Dublin, as people had to do formerly.

Many people are now eagerly studying these books and men often come to Ireland from France, Germany, Italy, Norway and Sweden, Russia, and other countries, in order to learn the Irish language so as to be able to read them. But this requires much study, even from those who know the Irish of the present day; for the language of those books is old and difficult.

In many National and Intermediate schools the Irish language is now taught, and no doubt some of the pupils who attend the Irish classes will continue[Pg 120]their studies after they leave school, till they come to be able to read our old books.

A great many old Irish tales and histories have been printed and translated, and some of them are very beautiful and instructive. Several of the stories in this book are from the Book of the Dun Cow and the Book of Leinster.

XXVII.

THE GILLA DACKER AND HIS HORSE.[34]

Once upon a time, when Finn and the Fena were hunting over Munster, Finn and some of his companions encamped on the slope of Knockainey hill[35]to rest for awhile. And they sent Finn Mac Bressal to the top of the hill to keep watch and ward, while they amused themselves, some playing chess, and some viewing the chase all round and listening to the sweet cry of the hounds.

Finn Mac Bressal had been watching only a little[Pg 121]time, when he saw on the plain to the east, a Fomor[36]of vast size coming towards the hill, leading a horse. As he came nearer, Finn Mac Bressal observed that he was the ugliest-looking giant his eyes ever lighted on. He had a large, thick body, bloated and swollen out to a great size; clumsy, crooked legs; and broad, flat feet, turned inwards. His hands and arms and shoulders were bony and thick and very strong-looking; his neck was long and thin; and while his head was poked forward, his face was turned up, as he stared straight at Finn Mac Bressal. He had thick lips, and long crooked teeth; and his face was covered all over with bushy hair.

He was fully armed; but all his weapons were rusty and soiled. A broad shield of a dirty, sooty colour, rough and battered, hung over his back; he had a long, heavy, straight sword at his left hip; and he grasped in his left hand two thick-handled, broad-headed spears, old and rusty, that looked as if they had not been handled for years. In his right hand he held an iron club, which he dragged after him, with its end on the ground; and it was so heavy that, as it trailed along, it tore up a track as deep as the furrow a farmer ploughs with a pair of oxen.

The horse he led was even larger in proportion than the giant himself, and quite as ugly. His great carcase was covered all over with tangled, scraggy-hair, of a sooty black; you could count his ribs and all the points of his big bones through his hide; his legs were crooked and knotty; his neck was twisted; and as for his jaws, they were so long and heavy that they made his head look twice too big for his body.

The giant held the horse by a thick halter, and seemed to be dragging him forward by main force, the animal was so lazy and so hard to move. Every now and then when the beast tried to stand still, the giant would give him a blow on the ribs with his big iron club, which sounded as loud as the thundering of a great billow against the rough-headed rocks of the coast. When he gave him a pull forward by the halter, the wonder was that he did not drag the animal's head away from his body; and, on the other hand, the horse often gave the halter such a tremendous tug backwards that it was equally wonderful how the arm of the giant was not torn from his shoulder.

Now it was not an easy matter to frighten Finn Mac Bressal; but when he saw the giant and his horse coming straight towards him in that wise, he was seized with such fear and horror that he sprang from his seat, and, snatching up his arms, he ran down the hill-slope with the utmost speed towards the king and his companions, whom he found sitting round the chess-board, deep in their game.

They started up when they saw him looking so scared; and, turning their eyes towards where he pointed, they saw the big man and his horse coming up the hill. The Fena stood gazing at him in silent wonder, waiting till he should arrive; but although he was no great way off when they first caught sight of him, it was a long time before he reached the spot where they stood, so slow was the movement of his horse and himself.

XXVIII.

THE FENA CARRIED OFF BY THE GILLA DACKER'S HORSE.

Patiently and in silence the Fena stood till the giant came up; when he bowed his head, and bended his knee, and saluted the king with great respect.

Finn addressed him; and having given him leave to speak, he asked who he was, and what was his name; also what was his profession or craft, and why he had no servant to attend to his horse—if, indeed, such an ugly old spectre of an animal could be called a horse at all.

The big man made answer and said, "King of the Fena, I will answer everything you ask me, as far as lies in my power. As to where I came from, I am a Fomor of the north; but I have no particular[Pg 124]dwelling-place, for I am continually travelling about from one country to another, serving the great lords and nobles of the world, and receiving wages for my service.

"In the course of my wanderings I have often heard of you, O king, and of your greatness and splendour and royal bounty; and I have come now to visit you, and to ask you to take me into your service for one year; and at the end of that time I shall fix my own wages, according to my custom.

"You ask me also why I have no servant for this great horse of mine. The reason of that is this: at every meal I eat, my master must give me as much food and drink as would be enough for a hundred men; and whosoever the lord or chief may be that takes me into his service, it is quite enough for him to have to provide for me, without having also to feed my servant.

"Moreover, I am so very heavy and lazy that I should never be able to keep up with a company on march if I had to walk; and this is my reason for keeping a horse at all.

"My name is the Gilla Dacker,[37] and it is not without good reason that I am so called. For there never was a lazier or worse servant than I am, or one that grumbles more at doing a day's work for his master. And I am the hardest person in the whole world to[Pg 125]deal with; for, no matter how good or noble I may think my master, or how kindly he may treat me, it is hard words and foul reproaches I am likely to give him for thanks in the end.

"This, O Finn, is the account I have to give of myself, and these are my answers to your questions."

"Well," answered Finn, "according to your own account, you are not a very pleasant fellow to have anything to do with; and of a truth there is not much to praise in your appearance. But things may not be so bad as you say; and, anyhow, as I have never yet refused any man service and wages, I will not now refuse you."

Whereupon the Gilla Dacker was taken into service among the warriors for a year.

Then the big man said:—"Now, as to this horse of mine, I find I must attend to him myself, as I see no one here worthy of putting a hand near him. So I will lead him to the nearest stud, as I am wont to do, and let him graze among your horses. I value him greatly, however, and it would grieve me very much if any harm were to befal him; so," continued he, turning to the king, "I put him under your protection, O king, and under the protection of all the Fena that are here present."

At this speech the Fena all burst out laughing, to see the Gilla Dacker showing such concern for his miserable, worthless, old skeleton of a horse.

Howbeit, the big man, giving not the least heed to their merriment, took the halter off the horse's head, and turned him loose among the horses of the Fena.

But now, this same wretched-looking old animal, instead of beginning to graze, as everyone thought he would, ran in among the horses of the Fena, and began straightway to work all sorts of mischief. He cocked his long, hard, switchy tail straight out like a rod, and, throwing up his hind legs, he kicked about on this side and on that, maiming and disabling several of the horses. Sometimes he went tearing through the thickest of the herd, butting at them with his hard, bony forehead; and he opened out his lips with a vicious grin, and tore all he could lay hold on, with his sharp, crooked teeth, so that none were safe that came in his way either before or behind. And the end of it was, that not an animal of the whole herd escaped, without having a leg broken, or an eye knocked out, or his ribs fractured, or his ear bitten off, or the side of his face torn open, or without being in some other way cut or maimed beyond cure.

At last he left them, and was making straight for a small field where Conan Mail's horses were grazing by themselves, intending to play the same tricks among them. But Conan, seeing this, shouted in great alarm to the Gilla Dacker, to bring away his horse, and not let him work any more mischief; and threatening, if he did not do so at once, to go himself[Pg 127]and knock the brains out of the vicious old brute on the spot.

80

But the Gilla Dacker took the matter quite coolly; and he told Conan that he saw no way of preventing his horse from joining the others, except some one put the halter on him and held him, which would, of course, he said, prevent the poor animal from grazing, and would leave him hungry at the end of the day. "But," said he to Conan, "there is the halter; and if you are in any fear for your own animals, you may go yourself and bring him away from the field."

Conan was in a mighty rage when he heard this; and as he saw the big horse just about to cross the fence, he snatched up the halter, and running forward with long strides, he threw it over the animal's head and attempted to lead him back. But in a moment the horse stood stock still, and his body and legs became as stiff as if they were made of wood; and though Conan pulled and tugged with might and main, he was not able to stir him an inch from his place.

He gave up pulling at last, when he found it was no use; but he still kept on holding the halter, while the big horse never made the least stir, but stood as if he had been turned into stone; the Gilla Dacker all the time looking on quite unconcernedly, and the others laughing at Conan's perplexity. But no one offered to relieve him.

At last Conan jumped up on the horse, and tried to urge him on, but all to no purpose: for the animal[Pg 128]never stirred. Another of the Fena now mounted behind him, and another, and another, till there were fourteen of them on the horse's back. Then the Gilla Dacker, suddenly tucking up his skirts, darted away from the Fena, and ran south-west with the speed of a swallow flying across a mountain side, or of a March wind sweeping over the plain. When the horse saw his master running, he stirred himself at once and followed him with equal speed, carrying off the whole fourteen men, and plunging and tearing along as if he had nothing at all on his back.

The men now tried to throw themselves off; but this, indeed, they were not able to do, for the good reason that they found themselves fastened firmly, hands and feet and all, to the horse's back. Moreover they found that their seat was not a comfortable one, for the old horse's backbone was rough and scraggy, and nearly as sharp as a saw.

And now Conan, looking round, raised his big voice, and shouted to Finn and the Fena, asking them were they content to let their friends be carried off in that manner by such a horrible, foul-looking old spectre of a horse.

Finn and the others, hearing this, instantly started off in pursuit, and for miles on miles they kept the Gilla Dacker and the horse in view, but were not able to overtake them. At last the horse and his master came to the shore of the sea in the west of Kerry, and without stop or stay they plunged forward,[Pg 129]moving over the waves the same as on the dry land: and just as the Fena arrived at the shore, they lost sight of them in the distance.

XXIX.

DERMOT O'DYNA AT THE WELL.

Great was the astonishment of the Fena, and great their dismay, on seeing their comrades carried off in this manner on the back of the big horse. And now they took counsel; and what they resolved on was, to send Dermot O'Dyna and a party of the Fena in a ship to search for their companions. And Dermot and the others went on board, and sailed to the west for many leagues, till they lost sight of the shores of Erin. At length they came to an island with steep cliffs all round, so high that its head seemed hidden in the clouds: and they saw by the tracks, that up the face of this cliff the horse had made his way. And it was agreed that Dermot O'Dyna should climb up and explore the island in quest of their comrades. Then Dermot put on his armour and his helmet, and took his shield, his two spears, and his sword: and leaning on the handles of the spears, he leaped with a light, airy bound on the nearest shelf of rock. Using his spears and his hands, he climbed from ledge to ledge, while his companions watched him anxiously[Pg 130]from below; till, after much toil, he measured the soles of his two feet on the green sod at the top of the rock. And when, recovering breath, he turned round and looked at his companions in the ship far below, he started back with amazement and dread at the dizzy height.

He now looked inland, and saw a beautiful country spread out before him:—a lovely, flowery plain straight in front, bordered with pleasant hills, and shaded with groves of many kinds of trees. It was enough to banish all care and sadness from one's heart to view this country, and to listen to the warbling of the birds, the humming of the bees among the flowers, the rustling of the wind through the trees, and the pleasant voices of the streams and waterfalls.

Making no delay, Dermot set out to walk across the plain. He had not been long walking when he saw, right before him, a great tree laden with fruit, over-topping all the other trees of the plain. It was surrounded at a little distance by a circle of pillar-stones; and one stone, taller than the others, stood in the centre near the tree. Beside this pillar-stone was a spring well, with a large, round pool as clear as crystal; and the water bubbled up in the centre, and flowed away towards the middle of the plain in a slender stream.

Dermot was glad when he saw the well; for he was hot and thirsty after climbing up the cliff. He stooped down to take a drink; but before his lips[Pg 131]touched the water, he heard the heavy tread of a body of warriors, and the loud clank of arms, as if a whole host were coming straight down on him. He sprang to his feet and looked round; but the noise ceased in an instant, and he could see nothing.

After a little while he stooped once more to drink; and again, before he had wet his lips, he heard the very same sounds, nearer and louder than before. A second time he leaped to his feet; and still he saw no one. He knew not what to think of this; and as he stood wondering and perplexed, he happened to cast his eyes on the tall pillar-stone that stood on the brink of the well; and he saw on its top a large, beautiful drinking-horn,[38] chased with gold and enamelled with precious stones.

"Now surely," said Dermot, "I have been doing wrong: it is, no doubt, one of the virtues of this well that it will not let any one drink of its waters except from the drinking-horn."

So he took down the horn, dipped it into the well, and drank without hindrance, till he had slaked his thirst.

XXX.

DERMOT O'DYNA FIGHTS THE WIZARD-CHAMPION, AND AFTER A TIME RESCUES HIS COMRADES.

Hardly had Dermot taken the horn from his lips, when he saw a tall wizard-champion coming towards him from the east, clad in a complete suit of mail, and fully armed with shield and helmet, sword and spear. A beautiful scarlet mantle hung over his armour, fastened at his throat by a golden brooch; he had a gold torque round his neck; and a broad circlet of sparkling gold was bended in front across his forehead, to confine his yellow hair, and keep it from being blown about by the wind.

As he came nearer, he increased his pace, moving with great strides; and Dermot now observed that he looked very wrathful. He offered no greeting, and showed not the least courtesy; but addressed Dermot in a rough, angry voice—

"Surely, Dermot O'Dyna, Erin of the green plains should be wide enough for you; and it contains abundance of clear, sweet water in its crystal springs and green bordered streams, from which you might have drunk your fill. But you have come into my island without my leave, and you have taken my drinking-horn, and have drunk from my well; and[Pg 133]this spot you shall never leave till you have given me satisfaction for the insult."

A torque [pronounced tork] of gold: a twisted collar for the neck. Golden torques were much used by kings and other rich people. Many torques are in the National Museum: but most of them are better made and twisted more closely than the one here represented.

So spoke the wizard-champion, and instantly advanced on Dermot with fury in his eyes. But Dermot was not the man to be terrified by any hero or wizard-champion alive. He met the foe half-way; and now, foot to foot, and knee to knee, and face to face, they began a fight, watchful and wary at first, but soon hot and vengeful, till their shields and helmets could scarce withstand their strong thrusts and blows. Like two enraged lions fighting to the death, or two strong serpents intertwined in deadly strife, or two great opposing billows thundering against each other on the ocean border; such was the strength and fury and determination of the combat of these two heroes.

And so they fought through the long day, till evening came, and it began to be dusk; when suddenly the wizard-champion sprang outside the range of Dermot's sword, and leaping up with a great bound, he alighted in the very centre of the well. Down he went through it, and disappeared in a moment before Dermot's eyes, as if the well had swallowed him up. Dermot stood on the brink, leaning on his spear, amazed and perplexed, looking after him in the water; but whether the hero had meant to drown himself, or that he had played some wizard trick, Dermot knew not.

He sat down to rest, full of vexation that the wizard-champion should have got off so easily. And what chafed him still more was that his companions knew nought of what had happened, and that when he returned, he could tell them nothing of the strange hero; neither had he the least token or trophy to show them after his long fight.

Dermot now began to think what was best to be[Pg 135]done; and he made up his mind to stay near the well all night, in the hope of finding out something further about the wizard-champion on the morrow.

He walked towards the nearest point of a great forest that stretched from the mountain down to the plain on his left; and as he came near, a herd of speckled deer ran by among the trees. poising his spear, he threw it with an unerring cast, and brought down the nearest of the herd.

Then, having lighted a fire under a tree, he skinned the deer and fixed it on long hazel spits to roast, having first, however, gone to the well, and brought away the drinking-horn full of water. And he sat beside the roasting deer to turn it and tend the fire, waiting impatiently for his meal; for he was hungry and tired after the toil of the day.

When the deer was cooked, he ate till he was satisfied, and drank the clear water of the well from the drinking-horn; after which he lay down under the shade of the tree, beside the fire, and slept a sound sleep till morning.

Night passed away and the sun rose, bringing morning with its abundant light. Dermot started up, refreshed after his long sleep, and, repairing to the forest, he slew another deer, and fixed it on hazel spits to roast at the fire as before. For

Dermot had this custom, that he would never eat of any food left from a former meal.

And after he had eaten of the deer's flesh and[Pg 136]drunk from the horn, he went towards the well. But though his visit was early, he found the wizard-champion there before him, standing beside the pillar-stone, fully armed as before, and looking now more wrathful than ever. Dermot was much surprised; but before he had time to speak, the wizard-champion addressed him—

"Dermot O'Dyna, you have now put the cap on all your evil deeds. It was not enough that you took my drinking-horn and drank from my well: you have done much worse than this, for you have hunted on my grounds, and have killed some of my speckled deer. Surely there are many hunting-grounds in Erin of the green plains, with plenty of deer in them; and you need not have come hither to commit these robberies on me. But now for a certainty you shall not go from this spot till I have taken satisfaction for all these misdeeds."

And again the two champions attacked each other, and fought during the long day, from morning till evening. And when the dusk began to fall, the wizard-champion leaped into the well, and disappeared down through it, even as he had done the day before.

The selfsame thing happened on the third day. And each day, morning and evening, Dermot killed a deer, and ate of its flesh, and drank of the water of the well from the drinking-horn.

On the fourth morning, Dermot found the wizard-champion standing as usual by the pillar-stone near the well. And as each morning he looked more angry than on the morning before, so now he scowled in a way that would have terrified anyone but Dermot O'Dyna.

And they fought during the day till the dusk of evening. But now Dermot watched his foe narrowly; and when he saw him about to spring into the well he closed on him and threw his arms round him. The wizard-champion struggled to free himself, moving all the time nearer and nearer to the brink; but Dermot held on, till at last both fell into the well. Down they went, clinging to each other, Dermot and the strange champion; down, down, deeper and deeper they went; and Dermot tried to look round, but nothing could he see save darkness and dim shadows. At length there was a glimmer of light; then the bright day burst suddenly upon them; and presently they came to the solid ground, gently and without the least shock.

At the very moment they reached the ground, the wizard-champion, with a sudden effort, tore himself away from Dermot's grasp, and ran forward with great speed. Dermot leaped to his feet; and he was so amazed at what he saw around him that he stood stock still and let the wizard-champion escape:—a lovely country, with many green-sided hills and fair valleys between, woods of red yew trees, and plains laughing all over with flowers of every hue.

Right before him, not far off, lay a city of great tall houses with glittering roofs; and on the side nearest to him was a royal palace, larger and grander than the rest. On the level green in front of the palace were a number of knights, all armed, and amusing themselves with various warlike exercises of sword and shield and spear.

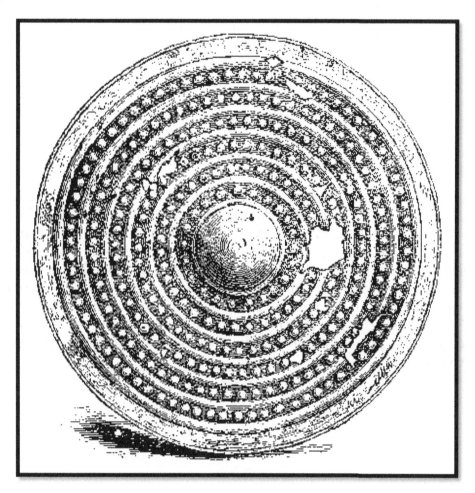

Ancient Irish bronze shield, 28 inches in diameter, found in a bog in the Co. Limerick. Shields were often made of yew-wood, which is very hard: and oftener still of wickerwork, covered outside with tough hides, generally tanned. Wickerwork shields were sometimes large

enough to cover the whole body. On the inside of every shield was a crossbar which was held in the hand: and for additional safety a leather strap fastened to the shield, went round the warrior's neck.

To tell all Dermot's adventures here would be too long for this book. But he remained in that[Pg 139]strange country, till he met the wizard champion and subdued him in fight. And after much searching he found Conan and the others who had been carried off by the Gilla Dacker's horse after which they all returned to the ship. And they sailed back to Erin where, when they landed, they were welcomed with a mighty shout by the assembled Fena.

From "Old Celtic Romances," by P. W. JOYCE, LL.D.

XXXI.

SAINT COLUMKILLE: PART I.

Saint Columkille[39] was born in the year 521, in Gartan, a wild district in the county Donegal, not far from Letterkenny. He was a near relation of the kings of Ireland of his time; for his father was great-grandson of the mighty King Niall of the Nine Hostages (see p. 5): and his mother was related to the kings of Leinster. He spent his boyhood in a little village near Gartan; and when he was old enough, he was sent away from his home to a school kept by a[Pg 140]distinguished bishop and teacher, St. Finnen, at Movilla, near the present Newtownards, in Down. Though he belonged to a princely family, and might easily have become rich and great, he gave up these worldly advantages for religion, and resolved to become a priest.

Ruins of the Monastery of Movilla, near Newtownards. (Drawn in 1845.)

Having spent some time at Movilla, the youthful Columkille went to several other Irish Colleges, including that of St. Movi, at Glasnevin, near Dublin; and as he was a diligent student, he made great progress in all. The most celebrated of these was at Clonard, in Meath, in which there were many hundreds of students under the instruction of another St. Finnen, a great and holy man, who is styled in old Irish writings "a doctor of wisdom and the tutor of the saints of Ireland in his time." Here Columkille met many young Irishmen who afterwards became distinguished saints and missionaries.

As soon as he was ordained priest, he set about the work of his life—spreading the Gospel. At that time the high ridge over the river Foyle, where now stands the old city of Derry, was anunin habited spot, clothed with a splendid wood of oaks, from which it got the name of Derry, meaning an oak grove: this spot was presented to Columkille by his cousin, prince Aed, afterwards king of Ireland. Here, when he was twenty-five years of age, he built his first church, round which grew up a monastery that continued to flourish for many hundred years, so that, in memory of the saint, the place was long afterwards known by the name of Derry-Columkille. At this period of his life he was a man of noble presence, a worthy member of a kingly race, as one of the old Irish writers describes him:— tall, broad-shouldered, and powerful: with long, curling hair:[Pg 142]luminous grey eyes, and a countenance bright and pleasing: and he was always lively and agreeable in conversation.

Remains of a Round Tower at Drumcliff, 4 miles north of Sligo town: built near the church founded by St. Columkille; but long after his time.

For fifteen years after the establishment of Derry, Columkille continued to found churches all over the country, among many others those of Kells in Meath, Tory Island, Swords near Dublin, Drumcliff in Sligo, and Durrow in King's County, the last of which was his chief establishment in Ireland. It is recorded that during these fifteen years he founded altogether three hundred churches and monasteries. These establishments, like all the other Irish monasteries, were the means of spreading not only religion but general enlightenment: for in most of them there were schools; and the priests and monks converted, and taught, and civilised, to the best of their power, the people in their neighbourhood.

Many years before this, St. Patrick and the missionaries who worked under his guidance, had converted the greatest part of the Irish people to Christianity. But the time was too short and the missionaries too few to instruct the newly-converted people fully in their faith: so that although they were Christians, many of them had only a poor knowledge of the Christian doctrine. In those times there were certain persons in Ireland called Druids, who were the learned men among the pagans of the day, and who taught the people the pagan religion known as Druidism. They hated the Christian faith, and gave St. Patrick and his companions great trouble by trying to persuade the pagan Irish not to become Christians. They continued in the country till the time of St. Columkille, as active as ever though much fewer; and St. Columkille and the other missionaries of his time had often hard work to win over the people from the false teaching of these druids, and make good Christians of them.

A great part of the north of Scotland was then inhabited by a people called the Picts. Those of them who lived south of the Grampian mountains had been converted some time before by St. Ninian of Glastonbury:[40] but the northern Picts were still pagans; and Columkille made up his mind to leave[Pg 144]Ireland and devote the rest of his life to their conversion. In 563, in the forty-second year of his age, he bade a sorrowful farewell to his native country, and crossing the sea with twelve companions, he settled in the island of Iona, in the Hebrides, which had been presented to him by his relative, the king of that part of Scotland. Here he built his little church and monastery, all of wood, and began to prepare for his glorious work. This little island afterwards became the Greatest religious centre in Scotland: and grand churches and other buildings were erected in and around the site of Columkille's humble structures. For many centuries Iona was held in such honour that most of the kings and chiefs and other great people of Scotland were buried in it; and to this day it is full of venerable and beautiful ruins, which are every year visited by people from all parts of the British Islands.

The most laborious part of St. Columkille's active life began after his settlement in Iona. He traversed the Highlands of Scotland and the Islands of the Hebrides, sometimes in a rude chariot, sometimes on foot, visiting the kings and chiefs of the Picts, and preaching to them in their homes; and he founded churches and monasteries all over that part of Scotland, just as he had done in Ireland. After many years of incessant labour he succeeded in converting the whole of the northern Picts.

When Columkille was at home in his monastery[Pg 145]resting from his missionary labours, his favourite occupation was copying the Holy Scriptures. We are told that he wrote with his own hand, in the course of years, three hundred copies of the sacred books, which he presented to the various churches he had founded; and this good work he continued to the very last day of his life. Besides mere copying, he composed many hymns and other poems, both in Latin and Irish. He was always employed at something. Adamnan says that not an hour of the day passed by without some work for himself and his monks—praying, reading, writing, arranging the affairs of the monastery, or manual work: for he took his own share in cooking, grinding corn, overseeing the men who were working in the fields, and so forth.

XXXII.

SAINT COLUMKILLE: PART II.

During St. Columkille's residence in Iona he visited Ireland more than once, on important business: and we may be sure that he was delighted when the opportunity came to see again the land he loved so well. The most important of these occasions was when he came over to take part in a great Meeting—a sort of Parliament for all Ireland—which was held at a place called Drum-Ketta in[Pg 146]Derry. The proceedings at this meeting will be found described in the "Child's History of Ireland."

Amidst all the earnest and laborious efforts of St. Columkille in the cause of religion, he never forgot his native country. He looked upon himself as an exile, though a voluntary exile in a great and glorious cause; and a tender regret was always mingled with his recollections of Ireland. We have in our old books a very ancient poem in the Irish language, believed to have been composed by him, in which he expresses himself in this manner:—

"How delightful to be on Ben-Edar beforeembarking on the foam-white sea: how pleasant to row one's little curragh all round it, to look upward at its bare steep border, and to hear the waves dashing; against its rocky cliffs.

"A grey eye looks back towards Erin: a grey eye full of tears.

"While I traverse Alban of the ravens, I think on my little oak grove in Derry. If the tributes and the riches of Alban were mine, from the centre to the utmost borders, I would prefer to them all one little house in Derry. The reason I love Derry is for its quietness, for its purity, for its crowds of white angels.

"How sweet it is to think of Durrow: how delightful would it be to hear the music of the breeze rustling through its groves.

"Plentiful is the fruit in the Western Island—beloved Erin of many waterfalls: plentiful her noble proves of oak. Many are her kings and princes; sweet-voiced her clerics; her birds warble joyously in the woods; gentle are her youths; wise her seniors; comely and graceful her women, of spotless virtue; illustrious her men, of noble aspect.

"There is a grey eye that fills with tears when it looks back towards Erin. While I stand on the oaken deck of my bark I stretch my vision westwards over the briny sea towards Erin."

During his whole life Columkille retained his affection for his native land and for everything connected with it. One breezy day, when he was now in his old age in Iona, a crane appeared flying towards the island: it was beaten about by the wind, and with much difficulty it reached the beach, where it fell down quite spent with hunger and fatigue. And the good old man said to one of his monks:—

"That crane has come from our dear fatherland, and I earnestly commend it to thee: nurse and cherish it tenderly till it is strong enough to return again to its sweet home in Scotia."

Accordingly the monk took the bird up in his arms and brought it to the hospice, and fed and tended it for three days till it had quite recovered. The third day was calm, and the bird rose from the earth till it had come to a great height, when resting for a moment to look forward, it stretched out its neck and directed its course towards Ireland.

Round Tower of St. Canice, Kilkenny: 100 feet high, and perfect, except that it wants the pointed cap. St. Canice was an intimate friend of St. Columkille: but this tower was not erected till some centuries after the death of the two saints.

On the day before the saint's death he went to a little hill hard by the monastery that overlooked the whole place; and gazing-lovingly round him for the last time, he lifted up his hands and blessed the monastery. And as he was returning with his attendant, he grew tired and sat down half way to rest; for he was now very weak. While he was sitting here an old white horse that was employed for many years to carry the pails between the milking place and the monastery, first looked at him intently, and then, coming up slowly, step by step, he laid his head gently on the saint's bosom. And he began to moan pitifully, and big tears rolled from his eyes and fell into the saint's lap: which, when the attendant saw, he came up to drive him away. Put the old man said:—"Let him alone: he loves me. May be God has given him some dim knowledge that his master is going; from him and from you all: so let him alone." At last, standing up, he blessed the poor old animal and returned to the monastery.

The death call came to him when he was seventy-six years of age. Though his death was not a sudden one, he had no sickness before it: he simply sank, wearied out with his life-long labours. Although he knew his end was near, he kept writing one of the Psalms till he could write no longer; while his companion Baithen sat beside him. At last, laying down the pen, he said, "Let Baithen write the rest."

On the night of that same day, at the toll of the midnight bell for prayer, he rose, feeble as he was, from his bed, which was nothing but a bare flagstone, and went to the church hard by, followed immediately after by his attendant Dermot. He arrived there before the others had time to bring in the lights; and Dermot, losing sight of him in the darkness, called out several times, "Where are you, father?" Perceiving no reply, he felt his way,[Pg 150]till he found his master before the altar kneeling and leaning forward on the steps: and raising him up a little, supported his head on his breast. The monks now came up with the lights; and seeing their beloved old master dying, they began to weep. He looked at them with his face lighted up with joy, and tried to utter a blessing; but being unable to speak, he raised his hand a little to bless them, and in the very act of doing so he died in Dermot's arms.[41]

XXXIII.

PRINCE ALFRED IN IRELAND.

It has been already stated (p. 47) that in early ages great numbers of foreigners came to Ireland to study in the colleges. Among those was Aldfrid or Alfred,[42] Prince of Northumbria, one of the Kingdoms[Pg 151]of the Saxon Heptarchy. His history is interesting to us as exhibiting an example of the class of persons who came to Ireland for education in those days, and as showing the close relations existing between many of the royal families of England and Ireland.

In the year 670, on the death of his father Oswy, who was king of Northumbria, the throne was seized unjustly by Alfred's younger brother, Egfrid: whereupon

Alfred fled to Ireland. He was all the more ready to choose this as his place of exile, inasmuch as he was fond of learning, and he knew well that there were more learned and skilful teachers and better opportunities for study in Ireland than elsewhere. But he had another good reason; for his mother Fina [Feena] was an Irish princess of the family of the kings of Meath. The Irish knew him by the name "Flann," or more commonly Flann Fina, from his mother. He remained many years in Ireland, studying with greatdiligence in various colleges, till he had mastered most of the branches of learning then taught. He became specially skilled in the Holy Scriptures, and he also learned to speak and write the Irish language.

While he was in Ireland he was for a time under the instruction of St. Adamnan, the writer of the life of St. Columkille (see p. 140, note); and so close and affectionate was the intimacy between them, that the ancient Irish writers often call Alfred Adamnan's foster-son.

In the year 684 a party of Saxons were sent from Northumbria by Egfrid across the sea on a plundering expedition to Ireland. Having ravaged the coast of Meath,[43] between Ben-Edar and the Boyne, thesemarauders carried off a number of captives, who were held in bondage during the short remainder of his reign. In the very next year Egfrid was killed in battle, on which the Northumbrian nobles, who were well aware of Alfred's virtues and great abilities, sent to Ireland inviting him to take the throne: and accordingly he returned to England and became king of the Northumbrians.

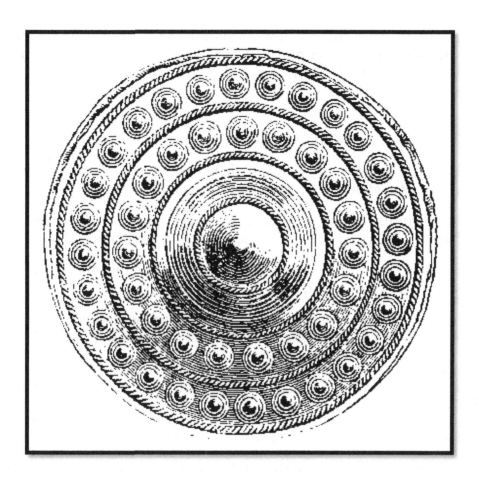

Ancient Irish thin plate of gold, twice the size of the picture. This is one of the bosses at the two ends of a gorget. Now in the National Museum, Dublin.

The poor captives were still kept in slavery: but Adamnan, seeing now a chance for their release, proceeded to the Northumbrian court to plead with his friend and former pupil for their restoration. He was received most affectionately; and at his intercession the king had the captives set free. Adamnan then brought them back, to the number of sixty, and restored them all rejoicing to their homes and friends.

As soon as Alfred had taken possession of the throne he took careful measures to have his people instructed in learning, religion, and virtue, in accordance with what he had himself seen and learned in Ireland; and he governed his kingdom for nineteen years in peace and prosperity.

In several ancient Irish manuscripts, including the Book of Leinster, there is a poem in the Irish language in praise of Ireland, said to have been composed by Alfred Flann Fina; of which the following are some of the verses faithfully translated[44]:—

PRINCE ALDFRID'S ACCOUNT OF IRELAND.

I found in Inisfail the fair, In Ireland, while in exile there, Women of worth, both grave and gay men, Many clerics and many laymen.

I travelled its fruitful provinces round, And in every one of the five I found, Alike in church and in palace hall, Abundant apparel, and food for all.

Gold and silver I found, and money, Plenty of wheat and plenty of honey; I found God's people rich in pity, Found many a feast and many a city.

I found in Munster, unfettered of any, Kings, and queens, and poets a many— Poets well skilled in music and measure, Prosperous doings, mirth and pleasure.

I found in Connaught the just, redundance Of riches, milk in lavish abundance; Hospitality, vigour, fame, In Cruachan's[45] land of heroic name.

I found in Ulster, from hill to glen, Hardy warriors, resolute men; Beauty that bloomed when youth was gone, And strength transmitted from sire to son.

I found in Leinster the smooth and sleek, From Dublin to Slewmargy's[46] peak; Flourishing pastures, valour, health, Long-living worthies, commerce, wealth.

I found in Meath's fair principality, Virtue, vigour, and hospitality; Candour, joyfulness, bravery, purity, Ireland's bulwark and security.

I found strict morals in age and youth, I found historians recording truth; The things I sing of in verse unsmooth, I found them all—I have written sooth.

XXXIV.

THE VOYAGE OF MAILDUNE.

AN ACCOUNT OF THE ADVENTURES OF MAILDUNE[47] AND HIS CREW, AND OF THE WONDERFUL THINGS THEY SAW DURING THEIR VOYAGE OF THREE YEARS AND SEVEN MONTHS, IN THEIR CURRAGH, ON THE WESTERN SEA.

In that part of Thomond[48] lying opposite the Aran Islands there once lived a young chief named Maildune. When he was an infant, a band of marauders landed on the coast, and plundered the whole district, and slew his father by burning the house over his head. Maildune grew up knowing nothing of all this, for his mother concealed it from him. But one day, when he was now a young man, he was contending in certain games of strength with a number of young persons of his own age, and he obtained the victory in every contest. At last it came to throwing the handstone: and when he had thrown it farther than all the others, an envious foul-tongued fellow who was standing by said to him:—

"It would better become you to avenge the man who was burned to death here, than to be amusing yourself casting a stone over his bare, burnt bones."

"Who was he?" inquired Maildune.

"Your own father," replied the other.

"Who slew him?" asked Maildune.

"Plunderers from a fleet slew him and burned him in this house; and the same plunderers are now living in an island far out in the sea, and they still have the same fleet."

Maildune was disturbed and sad after hearing this. He dropped the stone that he held in his hand, folded his cloak round him, buckled on his shield, and left the company. And having made further inquiry and found that the story was true, he resolved that he would never rest till he had overtaken these plunderers, and avenged on them the death of his father.

Then he sent for a skilful workman to whom he gave directions to make for him a triple-hide curragh[49] large enough to hold sixty persons and all things needed for a voyage. This was done: and Maildune chose his companions; and having laid in a little stock of provisions, and whatever other things were needed, he put to sea.

THE FIRST ISLAND.—TIDINGS OF THE PLUNDERERS.

They sailed that day and night, as well as the whole of the next day, till darkness came on again; and at midnight they saw two small bare islands, with two great houses on them near the shore. When they drew nigh, they heard the sounds of merriment and laughter, and the shouts of revellers intermingled with the loud voices of warriors boasting of their deeds. And listening to catch the conversation, they heard one warrior say to another—

"Stand off from me, for I am a better warrior than thou; it was I who slew Maildune's father, and burned the house over his head; and no one has ever dared to avenge it on me. Thou hast never done a great deed like that!"

"Now surely," said one of Maildune's companions to him, "Heaven has guided our ship to this place. Here is an easy victory. Let us sack this house, since our enemies have been revealed to us and delivered into our hands!"

While they were yet speaking, the wind arose, and a great tempest suddenly broke on them. And they were driven violently before the storm, all that night and a part of next day, into the great and boundless ocean; so that they saw neither the islands they had left nor any other land; and they knew not whither they were going.

Then Maildune said, "Take down your sail and put by your oars, and let the curragh drift before the wind in whatsoever direction it pleases God to lead us": which was done.

XXXV.

AN EXTRAORDINARY MONSTER.

During the next few days, the wind bore Maildune's curragh along smoothly, so that the crew had not to use their oars. The island they now came to had a wall all round it. When they approached the shore, an animal of vast size, with a thick, rough skin, started up inside the wall, and ran round the island with the swiftness of the wind. When he had ended his race, he went to a high point, and standing[Pg 159]on a large, flat stone, began to exercise himself according to his daily custom, in the following manner. He kept turning himself completely round and round in his skin, the bones and flesh moving, while the skin remained at rest.

When he was tired of this exercise, he rested a little; and he then set to work turning his skin continually round his body, down at one side and up at the other like a mill-wheel; but the bones and flesh did not move.

After spending some time at this sort of exercise, he started and ran round the island as at first, as if to refresh himself. He then went back to the same spot, and this time, while the skin that covered the lower part of his body remained without motion, he whirled the skin of the upper part round and round like the movement of a flat-lying millstone. And it was in this manner that he passed most of his time on the island.

Maildune and his people, after they had seen these strange doings, thought it better not to venture nearer. So they put out to sea in great haste. The monster, observing them about to fly, ran down to the beach to seize the curragh; but finding that they had got out of his reach, he began to fling round stones at them with great force and an excellent aim. One of them struck Maildune's shield and went quite through it, lodging in the keel of the curragh; after which the voyagers got beyond his range and sailed away.

In a wall-circled isle a big monster they found, With a hide like an elephant, leathery and bare ;He threw up his heels with a wonderful bound, And ran round the isle with the speed of a hare.

But a feat more astounding has yet to be told: He turned round and round in his leathery skin; His bones and his flesh and his sinews he rolled—He was resting outside while he twisted within!

Then changing his practice with marvellous skill, His carcase stood rigid and round went his hide; It whirled round his bones like the wheel of a mill—He was resting within while he twisted outside!

Next, standing quite near on a green little hill, After galloping round in the very same track, While the skin of his breast remained perfectly still, Like a millstone he twisted the skin of his back!

But Maildune and his men put to sea in their boat, For they saw his two eyes looking over the wall; And they knew by the way that he opened his throat, He intended to swallow them, curragh and all!

THE SILVER PILLAR OF THE SEA.

The next wonderful thing the voyagers came across was an immense silver pillar standing in the sea. It had eight sides, each of which was the width of an[Pg 161]oar-stroke of the curragh, so that its whole circumference was eight oar-strokes. It rose out of the sea without any land or earth about it, nothing but the boundless ocean; and they could not see its base deep down in the water, neither were they able to see the top on account of its vast height.

101

A silver net hung from the top down to the very water, extending far out at one side of the pillar; and the meshes were so large that the curragh in full sail went through one of them. When they were passing through it, Diuran, one of Maildune's companions, struck the mesh with the edge of his spear, and with the blow cut a large piece off it.

"Do not destroy the net," said Maildune; "for what we see is the work of great men."

"What I have done," answered Diuran, "is for the honour of my God, and in order that the story of our adventures may be more readily believed; and I shall lay this silver as an offering on the altar of Armagh, if I ever reach Erin."

That piece of silver weighed two ounces and a half, as it was reckoned afterwards by the people of the church of Armagh.

After this the voyagers heard someone speaking on the top of the pillar, in a loud, clear, glad voice; but they knew neither what he said, nor in what language he spoke.

XXXVI.

MAILDUNE MEETS HIS ENEMY, IS RECONCILEDTO HIM, AND ARRIVES HOME.

The next land the travelers sighted was a small island. On a near approach they recognised it as the very same island they had seen in the beginning of their voyage, in which they had heard the man in the great house boast that he had slain Maildune's father, and from which the storm had driven them out into the great ocean.

They turned the prow of their vessel to the shore, landed, and went towards the house. It happened that at this very time the people of the house were seated at their evening meal; and Maildune and his companions, as they stood outside, heard a part of their conversation.

Said one to another, "It would not be well for us if we were now to see Maildune."

"As to Maildune," answered another, "it is very well known that he was drowned long ago in the great ocean."

"Do not be sure," observed a third; "perchance he is the very man that may waken you up some morning from your sleep."

"Supposing he came now," asked another, "what should we do?"

The head of the house now spoke in reply to the last question; and Maildune at once knew the voice,[Pg 163]for it was the voice of the man who had made a boast of slaying the young chief's father.

And what he said was:—"I can easily answer that. Maildune has been for a long time suffering great afflictions and hardships; and if he were to come now, though we were enemies once, I should certainly give him a welcome and a kind reception."

When Maildune heard this he knocked at the door; and the door-keeper asked who was there; to which Maildune made answer—

"It is I, Maildune, returned safely from all my wanderings."

The chief of the house then ordered the door to be opened; and he went to meet Maildune, and brought him and his companions into the house. They were joyfully welcomed by the whole household; new garments were given to them; and they feasted and rested, till they forgot their weariness and their hardships.

They related all the wonders God had revealed to them in the course of their voyage, according to the word of the sage who says, "It will be a source of pleasure to remember these things at a future time."

After they had remained here for some days, Maildune and his companions returned to their own country. And Diuran took the piece of silver he had cut down from the great net at the Silver Pillar, and laid it, according to his promise, on the high altar of Armagh.

From "Old Celtic Romances," by P. W. JOYCE, LL.D.

XXXVII.

TENNYSON'S "VOYAGE OF MAILDUNE."

("FOUNDED ON AN IRISH LEGEND: A.D. 700.")

Of the tale called the "Voyage of Maildune," the oldest copy is in the Book of the Dun Cow, which was copied from older books eight hundred years ago: but here the story is imperfect at both the beginning and end, portions of the book having been torn away at some former time. There is, however, a perfect copy in the Yellow Book of Lecan.[50] It was translated and published for the first time in "Old Celtic Romances" in 1879. When this book appeared, the great English poet, Alfred Tennyson (afterwards Lord Tennyson), read the story, and made it the subject of a beautiful poem, also called "The Voyage of Maildune." Portions of the beginning and end of this poem are here given:—

I.

I was the chief of the race—he had stricken my father dead—But I gather'd my fellows together, I swore I would strike off his head. Each of them looked like a king, and was noble in birth as in worth,[Pg 165]And each of them boasted he sprang from the oldest race upon earth. Each was as brave in the fight as the bravest hero of song, And each of them liefer had died than have done one another a wrong. *He* lived on an isle in the ocean—we sail'd on a Friday morn—He that had slain my father the day before I was born.

II.

And we came to the isle in the ocean, and there on the shore was he.But a sudden blast blew us out and away thro' a boundless sea.

XI.

And we came to the Isle of a saint who had sail'd with St. Brendan[51] of yore, He had lived ever since on the Isle and his winters were fifteen score, And his voice was low as from other worlds, and his eyes were sweet,[Pg 166]And his white hair sank to his heels and his white beard fell to his feet, And he spake to me, "O Maeldune, let be this purpose of thine! Remember the words of the Lord when he told us 'Vengeance is mine! 'His fathers have slain thy fathers in war or in single strife, Thy fathers have slain his fathers, each taken a life for a life, Thy father had slain his father, how long shall the murder last? Go back to the Isle of Finn[52] and suffer the Past to be Past."

XII.

And we came to the Isle we were blown from, and there on the shore was he, The man that had slain my father. I saw him and let him be. O weary was I of the travel, the trouble, the strife and the sin, When I landed again, with a tithe of my men, on the Isle of Finn.

XXXVIII.

ST. DONATUS, BISHOP OF FIESOLE.[53]

PART I.

At page 47 of this book it has been related how missionaries and learned men went in great numbers from Ireland to the Continent in the early ages of Christianity to preach the Gospel and to teach in colleges. A full account of the lives and labours of these earnest and holy men would fill several volumes: but the following short sketch of one of them will give the reader a good idea of all.

Donatus was born in Ireland of noble parents towards the end of the eighth century. There is good reason to believe that he was educated in the monastic school of Inishcaltra, a little island in Lough Derg, near the Galway shore, now better known as Holy Island[54]: so that he was probably a native of that part of the country. Here he studied with great industry and success. He became a priest, and in course of time a bishop: and he was greatly distinguished as a professor.

Having spent a number of years teaching, he resolved to make a pilgrimage to Rome and visit the holy places on the way. He had a favourite pupil named Andrew, belonging to a noble Irish family, a handsome, high-spirited youth, but of a deeply religious turn: and these two, master and scholar, were much attached. And when Donatus made known his intention to go as a pilgrim to foreign lands, Andrew, who could not bear to be separated from him, begged to be permitted to go with him: to which Donatus consented. When they had made the few simple preparations necessary, they went down to the shore, accompanied by friends and relatives; and bidding farewell to all—home, friends, and country—amid tears and regrets, they set sail and landed on the coast of France.

And now, here were these two men, with stout hearts, determined will, and full trust in God, exhibiting an excellent example of what numberless Irish exiles of those days gave up, and of what trials and dangers they exposed themselves to, for the sake of religion. One was a successful teacher and a bishop; the other a young chief; and both might have lived in their own country a life of peace and plenty. But they relinquished all that for a higher and holier purpose; and they brought with them neither luxurynor comfort. They had, on landing, just as much money and food as started them on their journey; and with a small satchel strapped on shoulder, containing[Pg 169]a book or two and some other necessary articles, and with stout staff in hand, they travelled the whole way on foot. Whenever a monastery lay near their road, there they called, sure of a kind reception, and rested for a day or two. When no monastery was within reach, they simply begged for food and night shelter as they fared along, making themselves understood by the peasantry as best they could, for they knew little or nothing of their language. Much hardship they endured from hunger and thirst, bad weather, rough paths that often led them astray, and constant fatigue. They were sometimes in danger too from rude and wicked peasants, some of whom thought no more of killing a stranger than of killing a sparrow. But before setting out, the two pilgrims knew well the hardships and dangers in store for them on the way: so that they were quite prepared for all this: and on they trudged, contented and cheerful, never swerving an instant from their purpose. They travelled in a sort of zigzag way, continually turning aside to visit churches, shrines, hermitages, and all places consecrated by memory of old-time saints, or of past events of importance in the history of Christianity. And whenever they heard, as they went slowly along, of a man eminent for holiness and learning, they made it a point to visit him, so as to have the benefit of his conversation and advice; using the Latin language, which all learned men spoke in those times.

XXXIX.

ST. DONATUS, BISHOP OF FIESOLE:

PART II.

In this manner the pilgrims made their way right through France, and on through north Italy, till they arrived at Rome. This was the main object of their pilgrimage, and here they sojourned for a considerable time. Having obtained the Pope's blessing, they set out once more, directing their steps now towards Tuscany, till at length they reached the beautiful mountain of Fiesole, near Florence, where stood many churches and other memorials of Christian saints and martyrs. They entered the hospice of the monastery, intending to rest there for a week or two, and then to resume their journey. At this time Irish pilgrims and missionaries were respected everywhere on the Continent; and as soon as the arrival of those two became known, they were received with honour by both clergy and people, who became greatly attached to them for their gentle quiet ways, and their holiness of life.

It happened about the time of their arrival here, that the pastor of Fiesole, who was a bishop, died; and the clergy and people resolved to have Donatus for their pastor. But when they went to[Pg 171]him and told him what they wanted, he became frightened; and trembling greatly, he said to them in his gentle humble way:—

"We are only poor pilgrims from Scotia, and I do not wish to be your bishop; for I am not at all fit for it, hardly even knowing your language or your customs."

But the more he entreated the more vehemently did they insist: so that at last he consented to take the bishop's chair. This was in or about the year 824.

We need not follow the life of St. Donatus further here. It is enough to say that, notwithstanding all his fears and his deep humility, he became a great and successful pastor and missionary. For about thirty-seven years he laboured among the people of Fiesole, by whom he was greatly loved and revered. Down to the day of his death, which happened about 861, when he was a very old man, he was attended by his affectionate friend Andrew. He is to this day honoured in and around Fiesole, as an illustrious saint of those times. His tomb is still shown and regarded with much veneration: and in the old town there are several other memorials of him.

Like St. Columkille, Donatus always cherished a tender regretful love for Ireland; and like him also he wrote a short poem in praise of it which is still preserved. It is in Latin, and the following is a[Pg 172]translation, made by a Dublin poet many years ago:—

Far westward lies an isle of ancient fame, By nature bless'd; and Scotia is her name, Enroll'd in books[55]: exhaustless is her store, Of veiny silver, and of golden ore.[56]Her fruitful soil, for ever teems with wealth, With gems[57] her waters, and her air with health; Her verdant fields with milk and honey flow;[58]Her woolly fleeces[59] vie with virgin snow; Her waving furrows float with bearded corn; And arms and arts her envied sons adorn![60]No savage bear, with lawless fury roves, Nor fiercer lion, through her peaceful groves; No poison there infects, no scaly snake Creeps through the grass, nor frog annoys the lake;[61]An island worthy of its pious race, In war triumphant, and unmatch'd in peace!

XL.

HOW IRELAND WAS INVADED BY DANES AND ANGLO-NORMANS.

From the time of the settlement of the Milesians, as described at page 3, Ireland was ruled by native kings, without any disturbance from outside, till the arrival of the invaders we are now about to speak of.

During all these centuries, though there were troubles enough from the quarrels of the kings and chiefs, learning and art, as we have seen, were successfully cultivated. But a change came—a woful change—once the Danes began to arrive. These were pirates, all pagans, from Denmark and other countries round the Baltic Sea, brave and daring, but very wicked and cruel, who for a long period kept, not only Ireland, but the whole of western Europe in terror. They appeared for the first time on the coast of Ireland in the year 795, when they plundered St. Columkille's monastery on Lambay Island near Dublin. After this, for more than two hundred years, the country was never free from them, and they plundered and burned and destroyed churches, monasteries, libraries, and homesteads, and killed all that fell in their way, men, women, and children. They were often attacked and routed by the native chiefs; but this did not much discourage them and they generally landed so suddenly, and marched[Pg 174]through the country so swiftly, that in most cases they got clear off to their ships, with all their plunder, before the people could overtake them. They settled permanently in various towns on the coast, especially Dublin, Waterford, and Limerick, which they held for a long time.

At last they were overthrown by Brian Boru king of Ireland, in a great battle fought at Clontarf near Dublin, on Good Friday, the 23rd April, 1014, of which a full account may be read in the "Child's History of Ireland." After this, though no attempt was made to expel them from the country, they gave little trouble. They became Christians, intermarried with the natives, and settled down to industry and commerce like the rest of the people; and there are many of their descendants to this day in various parts of Ireland.

For about a century and a half after the battle of Clontarf, eight Irish kings reigned: but none of them succeeded in mastering the whole country. Some of these were O'Briens of Munster, the descendants of Brian Boru; some O'Loghlins of Ulster, a branch of the O'Neill family, descendants of Niall of the Nine Hostages (see p. 5); and some O'Conors of Connaught. During this period Ireland was greatly disturbed; for the several kings were continually fighting with each other, striving who should be head king: so that the next invaders, when they came, found the country ill prepared to resist them.

Those who have read the History of England will remember that the Normans, coming from France under William the Conqueror, took the sovereignty of England after the battle of Hastings in 1066. About a century later, their descendants, who were now called Anglo-Normans, i.e. English Normans, made settlements in Ireland. Their leader when they first arrived was Earl Strongbow; but in 1171 Henry II., king of England, came over with an army and took command. In 1172 he annexed Ireland to the crown of England, that is, he claimed it as a part of his dominions. The Over-king of Ireland at this time was Roderick O'Conor. He was unable to repel the new invaders: and after his death there was no longer a native king over all Ireland.

King Henry divided nearly the whole island among his lords, who all went, after some time, to reside in their own territories: but they were to remain under the authority of the king. These lords soon became great and powerful, and ruled like princes; and from them descend the chief Anglo-Irish families, of whom the most distinguished were the Geraldines or Fitzgeralds, the Butlers, and the De Burgos or Burkes.

But it must not be supposed that all this was done quietly: for the native Irish chiefs everywhere resisted these new lords. Although king Henry went through the form of "annexing" Ireland, it[Pg 176]was annexed only in name. In reality his authority extended over only a small portion. It took more than four hundred years to annex the whole country: and during all this time there were constant wars, the Anglo-Normans encroaching, and the Irish chiefs resisting as best they could. It was only in the reign of James I., that is, about three hundred years ago, that the whole of Ireland was brought under English law.

O'Dea's Castle, Dysart, Co. Clare. Built in the fourteenth century by one of the Irish chiefs.

Bunratty Castle in the south of Clare, on the Bunratty River, where it joins the Shannon: built about the end of the thirteenth century by Thomas de Clare, an Anglo-Norman lord.

These Anglo-Normans were a great and famous people, skilful and mighty in war; and they built splendid abbeys, churches, and castles, all over Ireland the ruins of which remain to this day. As an example of what manner of men they were, a sketch[Pg 178]of the career of one of them—Sir John de Courcy—is given in this book (page 190).

Kilclief Castle, Co. Down. Built by one of the Anglo-Normans in the fourteenth century.

For hundreds of years after the Invasion, people continued to come from England to live in Ireland both Anglo-Norman and Anglo-Saxon. After settling down they became good friends with the native Irish, intermarried with them, learned to speak and read the Irish language, and quite fell in with the customs and modes of the country, so that it was said of them that they became "more Irish than the Irish themselves." A large proportion of the present inhabitants of Ireland are of this race, mixed up however by intermarriage, with the older Milesian stock.

XLI.

THE WATCH-FIRE OF BARNALEE.

During the many wars in Ireland, small parties of men had often to traverse the country for long distances to bring messages from one general to another, and for other purposes. They marched by day and put up at night in the woods, choosing some sheltered corner and making a big fire of brambles to keep them warm and to cook their food. After supper they usually sat by the fire, amusing themselves with pleasant conversation or by telling stories: and when at last it was time to go to sleep, they wrapped themselves up in their great coats and lay down round the fire, leaving one of their number to stand guard.

The following short poem—part of a much longer one—describes how a small party of four men passed the early part of the night during a march across country. There was to be a battle in a day or two, and these four friends met, and each told a story by the Watch-fire of Barnalee. And they arranged to meet again after the battle, if any survived. But this turned out to be a sad meeting: there were only two: the other two lay dead on the battlefield.

I.

There were four comrades stout and free, Within the Wood of Barnalee, Under the spreading oaken tree.

II.

The ragged clouds sailed past the moon; Loud rose the brawling torrent's croon; The rising winds howled in the wood, Like hungry wolves at scent of blood. Yet there they sat, in converse free, Under the spreading oaken tree,—Garrod the Minstrel, with his lyre, Sir Hugh le Poer, that heart of fire, Dark Gilliemore, the mournful squire, And Donal, from the banks of nier.

III.

spectrally shone the watch-fire light On their sun-browned faces and helmets bright Showing beneath the woodland glooms Their swords, and jacks, and waving plumes; As there they sat, those comrades free, Within the Wood of Barnalee, Under the spreading oaken tree, And told their tales to you and me.

ROBERT DWYER JOYCE, M.D.

XLII.

113

CAHAL O'CONOR OF THE RED HAND:
KING OF CONNAUGHT.

Roderick O'Connor, the last native king of Ireland retired from the throne towards the end of the twelfth century, to end his days in the monastery of Cong.[62] After his time, as we have said, there was no longer a king over the whole country. But for hundreds of years afterwards, kings continued to reign over the five provinces. Roderick had been king of Connaught before he became king of all Ireland; and after his retirement there were several claimants for the Connaught throne, who contended with one another, so that the province was for a long time disturbed with wars and battles.

Roderick had a young brother named Cahal, who was called Cahal of the Red Hand, from a great blood-red mark on his right hand. He would naturally have a claim to the Connaught throne when old enough; and as he was, even when a boy, a noble young fellow, and showed great ability, the queen of Connaught, jealous of him, feared that when he grew up he would give trouble, and she sought him[Pg 182]out, determined to kill him: so that Cahal and his mother had to flee from one hiding place to another.

Finding at last that he could no longer remain in the province with safety, he and his mother crossed the Shannon into Leinster, where no one knew him, and there for several years they remained, while he made a poor living for both, by working in the fields as a common labourer. And as the fame of the brave young Cahal with the red mark on his hand, had gone abroad, he always wore a loose mitten on his right hand for fear of discovery; for he knew well that the queen had spies everywhere searching for him.

At this time the people had no newspapers: but there were news-carriers who made it their business to travel continually about the country, picking up information wherever they could, and relating all that occurred whenever they came to a village, or to any group of people who desired to hear the news. They generally received some small payment; and in this manner they made their living.

One day while Cahal was employed with several others, reaping in a field of rye, they saw one of these men approaching; and they stopped their work for a few moments to hear what he had to say. After relating several unimportant matters, he came at last to the principal news:—that the king of Connaught was dead, and that the leading people of the province, having met in counsel to choose a king[Pg 183]declared that they would have no one but young Cahal of the Red Hand. "And now," continued the newsman, "I and many others have been searching for him for several weeks. He is easily known, for his right hand is blood-red from

114

the wrist out: but up to this we have been unsuccessful. We fear indeed that he is living in poverty in some remoteplace where he will never be found: or it may be that he is dead."

When Cahal heard this, his heart gave a great bound, and he stood musing for a few moments. Then flinging his sickle on the ridge, he exclaimed:—"Farewell reaping-hook: now for the sword!" And pulling off the mitten, he showed his red hand, and made himself known. The newsman, instantly recognising him, threw himself prostrate before him to acknowledge him as his king. And ever since that time, "Cahal's farewell to the rye," has been a proverb in Connaught, to denote a farewell for ever. He returned immediately with his mother to Connaught, where he was joyfully received, and was proclaimed king in 1190.

At this time the Anglo-Norman barons who had come over at the time of Henry II.'s Invasion, nearly twenty years before, had settled down in various parts of Ireland: and they were constantly encroaching on the lands of the Irish and erecting strong castles everywhere; while the Irish chiefs as we have already said, resisted as far as they were[Pg 184]able, so that there was much disturbance all over the country. Cahal was a brave and active king, and took a leading part in fighting against the barons.

After he had reigned over Connaught in peace for eight or nine years, trouble came again. There was at this time, settled in Limerick, a powerful Anglo-Norman baron, William de Burgo, to whom a large part of Connaught had been granted by King Henry II. This man stirred up another of the O'Conors to lay claim to the throne in opposition to Cahal, promising to help him: and now Connaught was again all ablaze with civil war. Cahal was defeated in battle, and fled to Ulster to Hugh O'Neill, prince of Tyrone, who took up his cause. Marching south with his own and O'Neill's men, he attacked his rival, but was defeated, and again fled north. He soon made a second attempt, aided this time by Sir John de Courcy (for whom see page 190): but he and De Courcy were caught in an ambush in Galway by the rival king, who routed their army. In this fight De Courcy very nearly lost his life, being felled senseless from his horse by a stone. Recovering in good time however, he and Cahal escaped from the battlefield, and fled northwards.

Cahal of the Red Hand, in no way cowed by these terrible reverses, again took the field, after some time, aided now by De Burgo, who had changed sides. A battle was fought near Roscommon, in which the rival king was slain; and Cahal once[Pg 185]more took possession of the throne. From this period forward he ruled without a native rival; though a few years later, he was forced to surrender a large part of his kingdom to King John, in order that he might secure possession of the remainder.

But he was as vigilant as ever in repelling all attempts of the barons to encroach on his diminished territory. Thus when in 1220 the De Lacys of Meath, a most powerful Anglo-Norman family, went to Athleague on the Shannon at the head of Lough Ree, where there was a ford, and began to build a castle at the eastern or Leinster side, in order that they might have a garrison in it always ready to attack Connaught, Cahal promptly crossed the river into Longford, and so frightened them that they were glad to conclude a truce with him. And he broke down the castle, which they had almost finished.

Cahal of the Red Hand was an upright and powerful king, and governed with firmness and justice. The Irish Annals tell us that he relieved the poor as long as he lived, and that he destroyed more robbers and rebels and evil-doers of every kind than any other king of his time. In early life he had founded the abbey of Knockmoy,[63] into which he retired in the last year of his life: and in this retreat he died in 1224.

XLIII.

"CAHAL-MORE OF THE WINE-RED HAND."

The ancient Irish people—like those of several other countries—believed that when a just and good king reigned, the country was blessed with fine weather and abundant crops, the trees bended with fruit, the rivers teemed with fish, and the whole kingdom prospered. This was the state of Connaught while Cahal of the Red Hand reigned in peace. And it is recorded that when he died, fearful portents appeared, and there was gloom and terror everywhere. James Clarence Mangan, a Dublin poet, who died in 1849, pictures all this in the following fine poem. He supposes himself to be living on the river Maine, in Germany, and he is brought to Connaught in a vision, where he witnesses the prosperity that attended Cahal's reign. This he sets forth in the first part of the poem: but a sudden mysterious change for the worse comes, which he describes in the last two verses. The whole poem forms a wild, misty sort of picture, such as one might see in a dream.[64]

A VISION OF CONNAUGHT IN THE THIRTEENTH CENTURY.

I walked entranced Through a land of Morn; The sun, with wondrous excess of light, Shone down and glanced Over seas of corn And lustrous gardens a left and right. Even in the clime Of resplendent Spain, Beams no such sun upon such a land; But it was the time,'Twas in the reign, Of Cahal More of the Wine-red Hand.

Anon stood nigh By my side a man Of princely aspect and port sublime. Him queried I,"O, my Lord and Khan,[65]What clime is this, and what golden time?" When he—"The clime Is a clime to praise, The clime is Erin's, the green and bland; And it is the time, These be the days, Of Cahal More of the Wine-red Hand!"

[Pg 188]
Then saw I thrones, And circling fires, And a dome rose near me, as by a spell, Whence flowed the tones Of silver lyres, And many voices in wreathèd swell; And their thrilling chime Fell on mine ears As the heavenly hymn of an angel-band— "It is now the time, These be the years, Of Cahal More of the Wine-red Hand!"

I sought the hall, And, behold!... a change From light to darkness, from joy to woe! King, nobles, all, Looked aghast and strange; The minstrel-group sate in dumbest show! Had some great crime Wrought this dread amaze, This terror? None seemed to understand!'Twas then the time, We were in the days, Of Cahal More of the Wine-red Hand.

I again walked forth; But lo! the sky Showed fleckt with blood, and an alien sun Glared from the north, And there stood on high, Amid his shorn beams, A SKELETON[Pg 189]It was by the stream Of the castled Maine, One Autumn eve, in the teuton's land, That I dreamed this dream Of the time and reign Of Cahal More of the Wine-red Hand!

117

St. Finghin's Church, Quin, Co. Clare: originally built by the Irish: rebuilt by Thomas de Clare, the Anglo-Norman lord who erected Bunratty Castle (see p. 177). The Irish began to build large churches and castles a little before the arrival of the Anglo-Normans. The Irish churches of a previous time were generally small. After the Invasion, the Anglo-Norman barons and the Irish kings and chiefs vied with each other in erecting churches, abbeys, and castles.

XLIV.

SIR JOHN DE COURCY.

Among the many Anglo-Norman lords and knights who came to settle in Ireland in the time of Henry II., one of the most renowned was John de Courcy. The Welsh writer, Gerald Barry, already mentioned (p. 113), who lived at that time and knew him personally, thus describes him:—

"He was of huge size, tall and powerfully built, with bony and muscular limbs, wonderfully active and daring, full of courage, and a bold and venturous soldier from his youth. He was so eager for fighting that, though commanding as general, he always mingled with the foremost ranks in charging the enemy, which might have lost the battle; for if he chanced to be killed or badly wounded, there was no general able to take his place. But though so fierce in war, he was gentle and modest in time of peace and very exact in attending to his religious devotions; and when he had gained a victory he gave all the glory to God, and took none to himself."

When King Henry II. divided the country among his lords in 1172, he gave Ulster to De Courcy. But it was one thing to be granted the province, and another thing to take possession of it; for the Ulster chiefs and people were warlike and strong; and for[Pg 191]five years De Courcy remained in Dublin without making any attempt to conquer it.

At length he made up his mind to try his fortune; and gathering his followers to the number of about a thousand, every man well armed and trained to battle, he set out for the north. Through rugged and difficult ways the party rode on, and early in the morning of the fourth day—the 2nd February, 1177—they arrived at Downpatrick, then the capital of that part of the country. The Irish of those times never surrounded their towns with walls; and the astonished Downpatrick people, who knew nothing of the expedition, were startled from their beds at daybreak by a mighty uproar in the streets—shouts, and the clatter of horses' hoofs, and the martial notes of bugles. Whatever little stock of provisions the party had brought with them was gone soon after they left Dublin; and by the time they arrived at Downpatrick they were half-starved. They scattered themselves everywhere, and, breaking away for the time from the control of their leader, they fell ravenously on all the food they could lay their hands on: they smashed in doors and set fire to houses, and ate and drank and slew as if they were mad, till the town was half destroyed. And the people were taken so completely by surprise that there was hardly any resistance.

When this terrible onslaught at last came to an end, De Courcy, having succeeded in bringing his[Pg 192]men together, made an encampment, which he carefully fortified; and there the little army rested from their toils. At the end of a week the chief of the district came with a great army to expel the invaders; while De Courcy arranged his men in ranks with great skill, to withstand the attack. The Ulstermen who were without armour, wearing a loose saffron-coloured tunic over the ordinary dress, according to the Irish fashion, rushed on with fearless bravery; but by no effort could they break the solid ranks of the armour-clad Anglo-Normans, who, after a long struggle put them to flight, and pursued them for miles along the seashore.

After this victory De Courcy settled in Downpatrick with his followers, and built a strong castle there for his better security. Nevertheless the Ulstermen, in no way discouraged, continued their fierce attacks: and though he was victorious in several battles, he was defeated in others, so that for a long time he had quite enough to do to hold his ground.

But through all his difficulties the valiant De Courcy kept up his heart and battled bravely on, continually enlarging his territory, founding churches and building strong castles all over the province. King Henry was so pleased with his bravery, and with his success in extending the English dominions, that he made him earl of Ulster and lord of Connaught; and in 1185 he appointed him Lord Lieutenant of Ireland.[Pg 193]This obliged him to live in Dublin; but he left captains and governors in Ulster to hold his castles and protect his territory, till he should return, which he did in 1189.

XLV.

HOW SIR JOHN DE COURCY WAS CAPTURED AND THROWN INTO PRISON.

By the death of Henry II. in 1189, Sir John de Courcy lost his best friend: and things began to go ill with him when King John came to the throne in 1199. For another Anglo-Norman lord, Hugh de Lacy, grew jealous of his great deeds, and hated him with his whole heart, so that he took every means to poison the king's mind against him. In a very old volume, written by some Anglo-Irish writer, there are several entertaining stories of all that befel De Courcy after his return to Ulster from Dublin in 1189. Two of these, somewhat shortened and re-arranged, are given here, and much of the fine old language in which they are told is retained, as it is easily understood.

The first story relates that whereas Sir Hugh de Lacy, who was now appointed general ruler of Ireland by the king, did much disdain and envy Sir John de Courcy, and being marvellous grieved[Pg 194]at the worthy service he did, he sought all means that he could possible to damage and hinder him and to bring him to confusion, and promised much rewards in secret to those who would invent any matter against him; for which De Lacy had no cause but that Sir John's actions and commendations were held in greater account than his own. He feigned also false charges against him, and wrote them over to the king, and sore complained of him.

Amongst other his grievous complaints, he said De Courcy refused to do homage to King John, and he charged him also with saying to many that the king had somewhat to do with the death of Prince Arthur, lawful heir to the crown of England[66]; and many other such like things. All these were nothing but matters feigned by De Lacy, to bring to a better end his purpose of utterly ruining De Courcy. On this De Courcy challenged him, after the custom of those times, to try the matter by single combat: but De Lacy, fearing to meet him, made excuses and refused.

By reason of such evil and envious tales, though untrue they were, Sir Hugh de Lacy was at last commanded by King John to do what he might to apprehend and take Sir John de Courcy. Whereupon he devised and conferred with certain of Sir John's[Pg 195]own men how this might be done; and they said it was not possible to do so the while he was in his battle-harness. But they told him that it might be done on Good Friday; for on that day it was his accustomed usage to wear no shield, harness, or weapon, but that he would be found kneeling at his prayers, after he had gone about the church five times barefooted. And having so devised, they lay in wait for him in his church at Downpatrick; and when they saw him barefooted and unarmed they rushed on him suddenly. But he, snatching up a heavy wooden cross that stood nigh the church, defended him till it was broken, and slew thirteen of them before he was taken. And so he was sent to England, and was put into the Tower of London, to remain there in perpetual, and there miserably was kept a long time, without as much meat or apparel as any account could be made of.

Now these men had agreed to betray their master to Sir Hugh de Lacy for a certain reward of gold and silver: and when they came to Sir Hugh for their reward, he gave them the gold and silver as he had promised. They then craved of him a passport into England to tell all about the good service they had done; which he gave them, with the following words written in it:—

"This writing witnesseth that those whose names are herein subscribed, that did betray so good a master for reward, will be false to me and to all[Pg 196]the earth besides. And inasmuch as I put no trust in them, I do banish them out of this land of Ireland forever; and I do let Englishmen know that none of them may enjoy any part of this our king's land, or be employed as servitors from this forward forever."

Ennis Abbey as it appeared in 1780: now carefully preserved by the Board of Works. Built by Donogh O'Brien, king of Thomond, in 1242.

And so he wrote all their names, and put them in a ship with victuals and furniture, but without mariners or seamen, and put them to sea, and gave them strict charge never to return to Ireland on pain of death. And after this they were not heard of for a long time; but by chance of weather and lack of skilfull men, they arrived at Cork, and being taken, were brought to Sir Hugh de Lacy; and first[Pg 197]taking all their treasure from them, he hung them in chains, and so left them till their bodies wasted away.

This deed, that Sir Hugh de Lacy did, was for anen sample that none should use himself the like, and not for love of Sir John de Courcy: since it appeareth from certain ancient authors that he would have it so as that De Courcy's name should not be so much as mentioned, and that no report or commendation of him should ever be made.

XLVI.

SIR JOHN DE COURCY ACCEPTS A CHALLENGE.

And now Sir John de Courcy, being in the Tower in evil plight, cried often to God why He suffered him to be thus so miserably used, who did build so many good abbeys, and did so many good deeds to God: and thus often lamenting with himself, he asked God his latter end to finish.

It fortuned after this that much variance and debate did grow between King John of England and King Philip of France,[67] about a certain castle which the king of France won from King John. And when King Philip had often been asked to restore it[Pg 198]he refused, saying it was his by right. But at last he offered to try the matter by battle. For he had a champion, a mighty man, who had never been beaten; and he challenged the king of England to find, on his side, a champion to fight him, and let the title to the castle depend on the issue thereof; to which King John, more hasty than well advised, did agree.

And when the day of battle was appointed, the king of England called together his Council to find out where a champion might be found that would take upon him this honour and weighty enterprise. Many places they sought and inquired of, but no one was found that was willing to engage in so perilousa matter. And the king was in a great agony, fearing more the dishonour of the thing than the loss of the castle.

At length a member of the Council came to the king and told him that there was a man in the Tower of London, one De Courcy, that in all the earth was not his peer, if he would only fight. The king was much rejoiced thereat, and sent unto him to require and command him to take the matter in hand: but Sir John refused. The king sent again and offered him great gifts; but again he refused, saying he would never serve the king in field anymore; for he thought himself evil rewarded for such service as he did him before. The king sent to him a third time, and bade him ask whatever he would, for himself and for his friends,[Pg 199]and all should be granted to him: and he said furthermore that upon his stalworth and knightly doings the honour of the realm of England did rest and depend.

He answered that for himself, the thing he would wish to ask for, King John was not able to give, namely, the lightness and freedom of heart that he once had, but which the king's unkind dealing had taken from him. As for his friends, he said that, saving a few, they were all slain in the king's service; "and for these reasons," said he, "I mean never to serve the king more. But"—he went on to say—"the honour of the realm of England, that is another matter: and I would defend it so far as lies in my power, provided I might have such things as I shall ask for."

This was promised to him, and the king sent messengers to set him at liberty; who, when they had entered into his prison, found him in great misery. His hair was all matted, and overgrew his shoulders to his waist; he had scarce any apparel, and the little he had fell in rags over his great body; and his face was hollow from close confinement and for lack of food.

After all things that he required had been granted to him, he asked for one thing more, namely, that his sword should be sent for all the way to Downpatrick in Ireland, where it would be found within the altar of the church; for with that weapon he said he would fight and with no other. After much delay it was brought to him; and when they saw it and felt its weight, they marvelled that any man could wield it. And good food was given to him, and seemly raiment, and he had due exercise, and in all things he was cherished and made much of; so that his strength of body and stoutness of heart returned to him.

XLVII.

SIR JOHN DE COURCY AND THE FRENCH CHAMPION.

The lists were enclosed and all things were prepared against the day of battle. The two kings were there, outside the lists, with most of their nobility, and thousands of great people to look on, all sitting on seats placed high up for good view. Within the lists were two tents for the champions, where they might rest till the time appointed. And men were chosen to see that all things were carried on fairly and in good order.

When the time drew nigh, the French champion came forth on the field, and did his duty of obeisance, and bowed with reverence and courtesy to all around, and went back to his tent, where he waited for half an hour. The king of England sent for Sir John to come forth, for that the French champion rested a[Pg 201]long time awaiting his coming; to which he answered roughly that he would come forth when he thought it was time. And when he still delayed, the king sent one of his Council to desire him to make haste, to which he made answer:—"If thou or those kings were invited to such a banquet, you would make no great haste coming forth to partake of it."

On this the king, deeming that he was not going to fight at all, was about to depart in a great rage, thinking much evil of Sir John de Courcy. While he was thus musing, Sir John came forth in surly mood, for memory of all the ill-usage that had been wrought on him; and he stalked straight on, looking neither to the right nor to the left, and doing no reverence to anyone: and so back to his tent.

Then the trumpets sounded the first charge, for the champions to approach. Forth they came, and passing by slowly, viewed each other intently without a word. And when the foreign champion noted De Courcy's fierce look, and measured with his eyes his great stature and mighty limbs, he was filled with dread and fell all a-trembling. At length the trumpets sounded the last charge for the fight to begin; on which De Courcy quickly drew his sword and advanced; but the Frenchman, turning right round, "ranne awaie off the fielde and betooke him to Spaine."

Whereupon the English trumpets sounded victory; and there was such shouting and cheering, such[Pg 202]a-clapping of hands and such a-throwing of caps in the air as the like was never seen before.

When the multitude became quiet, King Philip desired of King John that De Courcy might be called before them to give a trial of his strength by a blow upon a helmet: to which De Courcy agreed. They fixed a great stake of timber in the ground, standing up the height of a man, over which they put a shirt of mail, with a helmet on top. And when all was ready, De Courcy, drawing his sword, looked at the kings with a grim and terrible look that fearful it was to behold; after which he struck such a blow as cut clean through the helmet and through the shirt of mail, and down deep in the piece of timber. And so fast was the sword fixed that no man in the assembly, using his two hands with the utmost effort, could pluck it out; but Sir John, taking it in one hand, drew it forth easily.

The princes, marveling at so huge a stroke, desired to understand why he looked so terrible at them before he struck the blow: on which he answered:—

"I call St. Patrick of Down to witness, that if I had missed the mark I would have cut the heads off both of you kings on the score of all the ill-usage I received aforetime at your hands."

King John, being satisfied with all matters as they turned out, took his answer in good part: and he gave him back all the dominions that before he had[Pg 203]in Ireland, as Earl of Ulster and lord of Connaught; and licensed him to return, with many great gifts besides. And to this day the people of Ireland hold in memory Sir John de Courcy and his mighty deeds; and the ruins of many great castles built by him are to be seen all over Ulster.

XLVIII.

THE GREAT EARL OF KILDARE AND THE EARL OF ORMOND.

The great lords who settled in Ireland in the time of Henry II. became so powerful that they ruled in the land like so many kings. It was so hard to reach Ireland in those times, or even to get from one part of Ireland to another, that their master, the king of England, had generally very little control over them: and he often found it hard enough even to find out what was going on among them. So those mighty barons did very much as they liked. They imposed taxes, raised armies, and made war on each other, just as if they were independent sovereigns.

The Fitzgeralds, or Geraldines, were among the most illustrious of those families. They intermarried with the families of the native Irish kings and princes, such as the O'Neills and O'Conors; and altogether they fell in so well with the ways of the country, that the Irish people came to love them almost better than they loved their own old native kings and chiefs. And for hundreds of years those Geraldines took a leading part in the government of Ireland for the kings of England.

In the time of Henry VII., who became king in the year 1485, Garrett Fitzgerald, earl of Kildare—the "Great Earl" as he was called—was Lord Deputy, or chief ruler of Ireland, for the king: and he was the leading man of his day in Ireland.[68] We

126

are told in the old accounts of him that he was tall of stature, of goodly presence, very liberal and merciful; of strict piety; mild in his government; very easily put into a passion, but just as easily appeased; a knight in valor, and princely in his words and judgments.

Once he got into a great rage with one of his servants for some blunder. It happened that two of the gentlemen of his household were looking on: and one of them whispered to the other, whose name was Boice, that he would give him a good Irish hobby if he went and plucked a hair out of the earl's beard. Boice took him at his offer, and knowing well the earl's good nature, he went up to him, while he still fumed with anger, and said:—

"If so it pleases your good lordship, one of your horsemen promised me a choice horse if I snip one[Pg 205]hair from your beard." "Well," quoth the earl, "I agree thereto; but if you pluck more than one, I promise you to bring my fist away from your ear!"

And Boice plucked the hair, and won the hobby: but he took good care to pluck only one, so that his ear escaped the earl's big fist.

At this time the chief man of the Butlers was James, earl of Ormond: and he and the Deputy were at enmity, each working with might and main to put down the other. The earl of Ormond, who was a deep and far reaching man, not being strong enough to oppose his adversary openly, devised a plan to entrap him by means of submission and courtesy. Certain charges had, it seems, been made against Ormond, and he now wrote to the deputy, who was, of course, in authority over him, asking permission to come to Dublin to disprove them; which the deputy granted. Accordingly, in the year 1492, he marched to Dublin with a numerous army, and encamped near the city.

Now Kildare's councillors, and the citizens in general, disliked the presence of so great an army, suspecting some evil design: and besides, the soldiers used the people ill, often beating and robbing them; so that instead of peace, this visit of Ormond made all the greater discord. Yet still, with an air of great respect and humility, he persisted in asking to be heard, saying he would show that the evil stories about him were all false. At length, Lord[Pg 206]Deputy Kildare agreed, and the meeting was held in St. Patrick's Church.

But this meeting was not a quiet or peaceful one; for the two earls, instead of speaking gentle words of forgiveness, began to accuse each other of all the damages inflicted on both sides. The citizens too, who were in great crowds around the church, complained with loud voices of all the ill-usage they had suffered from the soldiers; whereupon they and the soldiers fell to jars and quarrels, and the whole city was soon in an uproar. At last, a body of Dublin archers, enraged that such a disturbance should be raised by "this lawless rabble," rushed into the church, shouting out that they would kill Ormond, as the leader of them, and they shot at random hither and thither, leaving their arrows sticking in the timbers and ornaments of the church, but doing no harm otherwise. It is probable, indeed, that out of respect to the place, notwithstanding their rage, they took care to shoot over the heads of the crowd, so as to kill no one.

On this, the Earl of Ormond, fearing with good reason for his safety, fled with a few of his followers to the chapter-house, and slamming the door, bolted and barred it strongly. Kildare followed and called to him to come out, promising upon his honor that he should receive no harm. Ormond replied that he would come forth if the deputy gave him his hand that his life should be safe; so "a cleft was[Pg 207]pierced in a trice through the chapter-house door," to the end that the earls might shake hands and be reconciled. But Ormond, still suspecting treachery, refused to put forth his hand, fearing it might be chopped off, till at last Kildare stretched in his arm to him through the hole, and they shook hands. Then the door was opened and the two earls embraced, and the storm was appeased.

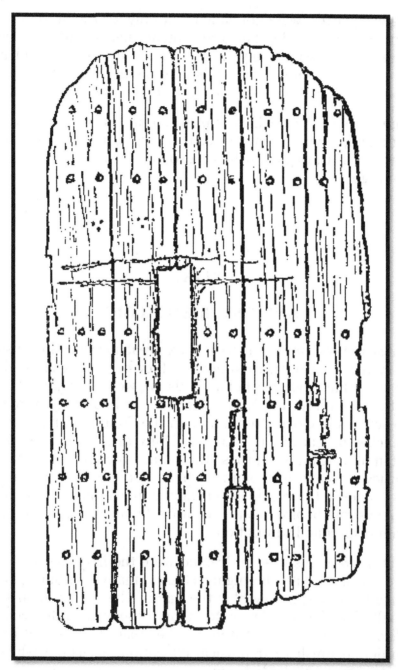

Old Chapter-house Door, now in St. Patrick's Cathedral, Dublin.

But though this quarrel was patched up, it was only for the time. Kildare suspected that Ormond had brought his army with evil intent "to outface him and his power in his own country"; while "Ormond mistrusted that this treacherous practice of the Dublinians was by Kildare devised." So that, as the old writer goes on to say, "their quarrels were not ended, but only for the present discontinued: like unto a green wound, rather bungerlie botcht, than sound lie cured. And these and the like surmises, with many stories carried to and fro, and in their ears whispered, bred and fostered a malice betwixt[Pg 208]them and their posterity, many years incurable, which caused much stir and unquietnesse in the realm."

The old chapter-house door, which is pictured on last page, still remains in St. Patrick's Cathedral, where it may be seen leaning against one of the walls, with the very "cleft" in it through which the two earls shook hands more than four hundred years ago.

XLIX.

ANCIENT IRISH MUSIC.

From the most remote times the Irish took great pleasure in music: and they studied and cultivated it so successfully that they became celebrated everywhere for their musical skill. Irish teachers of this art were thought so highly of that from about the seventh to the eleventh century, or later, they were employed in colleges and schools in Great Britain and on the Continent, like Irish professors of other branches of learning (see p. 47). Many of the early missionaries took great delight in playing on the harp, so that some brought a small harp with them on their journeys through the country, which no doubt lightened many a weary hour at their homes in the evenings, during the time of hard missionary work. In our oldest manuscript books, music is continually mentioned: and musicians are spoken of with respect and admiration.

The two chief instruments used in Ireland were the harp and the bagpipe. The harp was the favourite with the higher classes, many of whom played it as an accomplishment, as people now play the piano. The professional Irish harpers were more skillful, and could play better, than those of any other country: so that for hundreds of years it was the custom for the musicians of Great Britain to visit Ireland in order to finish their musical education; a custom which continued down to about a century and a-half ago.

The bagpipe was very generally used among the lower classes of people. The form in use was what we now call the Highland or Scotch pipes—slung from the shoulder: the bag inflated by the mouth. But this form of pipes took its rise in Ireland: and it was brought to Scotland in early ages by those Irish colonists already spoken of (page 5). There is another and a better kind of bagpipes, now common in Ireland, resting on the lap when in use, and having the bag inflated by a bellows: but this is a late invention.

The Irish musicians had various "*Styles,*" three of which are very often mentioned in tales and other ancient Irish writings: of these many specimens have come down to the present day. The style they called "Mirth-music" consisted of lively airs, which excited to merriment and laughter. These are represented by our present dance tunes, such as jigs,[Pg 210]reels, hornpipes, and other such quick, spirited pieces which are known so well in every part of Ireland. The "Sorrow-music" was slow and sad, and was always sung on the occasion of a death. We have many airs belonging to this style, which are now commonly called *Keens*, i.e., laments, or dirges. The "Sleep-music" was intended to produce sleep; and the tunes belonging to this style were plaintive and soothing. Such airs are now known as lullabies, or nurse tunes, or cradle songs, of which numerous examples are preserved in collections of Irish music. They were often sung to put children to sleep. Though there are, as has been said, many tunes belonging to these three classes, they form only a small part of the great body of Irish music.

Music entered into many of the daily occupations of the people. There were special spinning-wheel songs, which the women sang, with words, in chorus or in dialogue, when employed in spinning. At milking time the girls were in the habit of chanting a particular sort of air, in a low gentle voice. These milking songs were slow and plaintive, something like the nurse tunes, and had the effect of soothing the cows and of making them submit more gently to be milked. This practice was common down to fifty or sixty years ago; and many people now living can remember seeing cows grow restless when the song was interrupted, and become again quiet and placid when it was resumed. While ploughmen were at[Pg 211]their work they whistled a sweet, slow, and sad strain, which had as powerful an effect in soothing the horses at their hard work as the milking songs had on the cows: and these also were quite usual till about half a century ago.

Special airs and songs were used during working time by smiths, by weavers, and by boatmen. There were besides, hymn tunes; and young people had simple airs for all sorts of games and sports. In most cases words suitable to the several occasions were sung with lullabies, laments, and occupation tunes. The poem at page 82 may be taken as a specimen of a lament. Examples of all the preceding classes of melodies will be found in the collections of Irish airs by Bunting, Petrie, and Joyce.

The Irish had numerous war-marches, which the pipers played at the head of the clansmen when marching to battle, and which inspired them with courage and dash for the fight. This custom is still kept up by the Scotch; and many fine battle-tunes are printed in Irish and Scotch collections of national music.

From the preceding statement we may see how universal was the love of music in former days among the people of Ireland. Though Irish airs, compared with the musical pieces composed in our time, are generally short and simple, they are constructed with such skill, that in regard to most of them it may be truly said that no composer of the[Pg 212]present day can produce airs of a similar kind to equal them.

There are half a dozen original collections of Irish music, containing in all between 1000 and 2000 airs: other collections are mostly copied from these. But numerous airs are still sung and played among the people all through Ireland, which have never been written down; and many have been written down which have never been printed. Thomas Moore composed his beautiful songs to old Irish airs; and his whole collection of songs and airs—well known as "Moore's Melodies"—is now published in one small cheap volume.

Of the entire body of Irish airs that are preserved, we know the authors of not more than about one tenth; and these were composed within the last 200 years. Most of the remaining nine tenths have come down from old times. No one now can tell who composed "The Coolin," "Savourneen Dheelish," "Shule Aroon," "Molly Asthore," "Garryowen," "The Boyne Water," "Patrick's Day," "Langolee," "The Blackbird," or "The Girl I left behind me"; and so of many other well-known and lovely airs.

The national music of Ireland and that of Scotland are very like each other, and many airs are common to both countries: but this is only what might be expected, as we know that the Irish and the Highland Scotch were originally one people.

NOTES AND EXPLANATIONS.

I.
Ancient, very old, belonging to old times.
Fabulous, not true.
Magician, one skilled in magic or witchcraft; an enchanter.
Spell, a charm, something done by enchantment.
Wizard, an enchanter, a magician.
Consult, to advise with.
Druid, The druids were the learned men among the pagan Irish: they were believed to be wizards, or magicians.
Seer, one who can foresee events, a prophet.

Destiny, lot, what is to come to pass.
Wistfully, thoughtfully, attentively, longingly.
Cairn, a great pile of stones heaped up in memory of some person or some event. A cairn was very often raised over the grave of some important person.
Missionary, one sent to preach religion.
Hostage, a person given as a pledge, or security, for carrying out some agreement.
Possessing mighty power over people, able to persuade them by his earnestness and his powerful language.
II..
Gallantly, boldly, bravely.

Destined home: the druid had foretold that Inisfail, or the Isle of Destiny, was to be their final home.

Emerald, a precious stone of a green colour. Ireland, from its greenness, is often called the Emerald Isle.

Day god, the sun. Some of the pagan Irish worshipped the sun.

Omen, a sign of what is to come.

III.

Perpetual, lasting always.

Allure, to entice, coax, or persuade.

Book of the Dun Cow:

Conn the Hundred-fighter, or, as he is often called, Conn of the Hundred Battles, was King of Ireland from A.D. 177 to 212.

Crystal, a sort of transparent mineral: glass, or anything like glass.

Marvelled, wondered.

Chant, a slow, sweet song.

Azure, a bright blue.

Verdurous, green, full of verdure.

Imprecation, a curse.

Mace, here means a heavy-headed club used in fighting, generally for striking.

IV..

Noxious, hurtful, injurious.

Gigantic, very large, giant-like.

Fertile, fruitful, yielding good crops.

Wickerwork, basket-work of woven twigs.

Hospitality, kindness to strangers, free and generous entertainment of visitors.

Expensive, costly.

Establishment, the whole house, and all belonging to it.

Liberal, plentiful.

Gorget, an ornamental collar for the neck: the Irish gorgets were mostly of gold.

Bronze, a mixed metal made of copper and tin melted together. The ancient Irish used a sort of white or whitish bronze, which they called *findruine* [*finn´-drin-ă*].

Enamel, a beautiful glassy substance, of various colours, used in metal work.

Museum, a place where curiosities of all kinds are kept, especially objects belonging to ancient times.

[Pg 214]

Artificer, an artist, a worker in metals, bone, wood, &c.

Old Irish Laws: these were called the Brehon Laws.

Commerce, trade with foreign nations.

V.—Page 22.

Enmity, hatred, malice, ill feeling.

Gall, bitterness and sourness of heart.

Treachery, breach of faith, wickedness.

Chariot, a kind of carriage.

Druidical, made by the druids, who were believed to be enchanters, like the Dedannans.

Clamorous, noisy, screaming.

Repented, grew sorry.

Gaelic speech, the Irish language, which all the people of Ireland then spoke.

Plaintive, sad.

Lay, a song, a poem.

A husk of gore, withered up with grief.

Anguish, great trouble and misery.

Anthem, a song, a hymn: anthem of praise, *i.e.* of praise to God.

VI.—Page 27.

Amazement, astonishment, wonder.

Horror, terror mixed with dislike.

Lamentation, great sorrow.

Malignant, full of evil and badness.

Adventurous, spirited, daring, courageous.

Abhor, to hate, to detest, to have a horror of.

Transform, to change the form or shape.

Society, company.

The dreadful day of doom, "that day of woe," *i.e.* the Day of Judgment. The children of Lir had some obscure foreknowledge of the coming of Christianity.

Desolate, waste and solitary.

Tempestuous, stormy.

VII.

Abode, a dwelling.

Plight, an evil and unpleasant state.

Endure, to bear, to suffer.

Chain of repose: as if the breezes were bound down and kept at rest by a chain.

Darkness: the darkness of paganism.

Pure light, and Day star: Christianity.

Wreathed, twisted, curled.

Hazel-mead, a kind of mead with hazel nuts put into it to flavour it.

Lullaby, a nurse song: a song to put a person to sleep; see p.210.

Mannanan, or Mannanan Mac Lir, a Dedannan chief, the Pagan Irish god of the sea.

Angus, a Dedannan or fairy chief, who had his palace under one of the great mounds on the Boyne between Drogheda and Slane.

VIII.

Matin time, very early in the morning: before day: the time of first prayer.

Anchoret, a hermit.

Matins, very early morning prayers.

Transformed, changed, turned.

Waxed, grew, became: waxed very wroth, became very angry.

Cleric, a clergyman.

Radiant, bright, joyful, happy looking.

Lament, a sort of sad song.

IX.—Page 45.

Enlightenment, knowledge, education, intelligence.

Community, a number of persons living together in the same dwelling or in the same place.

Encounter, to meet with, to go against.

Interpreter, a person who explains in one language what a speaker says in another. The interpreter has to know both languages.

X.—Page 50.

Rampart, a wall or high bank for defence.

Structure, a building.

Household, all the people that live in one house.

Standard, a pole with a flag, banner, or colours, on top.

Transfer, to change from one to another.

Romantic stories, tales of fictitious adventures.

Diadem, a crown, or a band like a crown, worn round the head.

Spell of feebleness, weakness brought on by some sort of enchantment.

[Pg 215]

XI.—Page 55.

Pondering, thinking deeply.

Meet, fit, proper, becoming.

Ultonians, the Ulstermen.

Gainsay, to speak against, to contradict.

Ridge of the world, a usual expression in Irish writings.

Gracious, kind and gentle in manner.

Attendant, a person who attends, a servant.

Military service, service as soldiers under pay.

Betimes, in good time, early.

Booth, a hut or tent.

XII..

Pledge, security.

Submission, yielding, coming under a person's authority.

Knighthood. Knight, a soldier of high dignity: a champion: knighthood, the dignity of a knight. The ancient Irish often received knighthood at seven years of age.

Obligation, a promise, a bond, something one is bound to do.

Galley, a low flat vessel with oars and sails.

Chessboard, a board with black and white squares on which chess was played. The ancient Irish were very fond of chess.

Re-assure, to make a person sure that things are right, to encourage.

XIII.

Resort, to go often to a place.

Curragh, a light boat made of wickerwork covered with hides.

Persist, to continue without ceasing.

Perplexity, doubt, anxiety of mind.

Clan, a number of families or a race of people all more or less related to each other.

Slieve Fuad, a mountain near Newtownhamilton in Armagh: the name is now forgotten.

Baleful, evil, very bad or wicked.

Disaster, mishap, misfortune.

Meditate, to plan, to intend.

Handwood, a piece of wood to serve as a knocker, kept in a niche outside the door.

Battalion, a body of foot soldiers.

Alluring, very good, tempting a person to eat.

Viands, food, victuals.

XIV..

Looming, appearing darkly and dimly in the distance.

Steadfast, firm, fixed, determined.

Valorous, brave, fearless, valiant.

Your dear charge, Deirdre.

Assailants, persons assailing or attacking.

Misgivings, doubts and fears of something wrong.

Unwittingly, without knowing.

Unerring, with a straight aim so as not to miss.

XV.—Page 75.

Hireling troops, soldiers serving for pay: they were not Ultonians and did not belong to the Red Branch. The troops of the Red Branch could not be got to attack the Sons of Usna.

Shouts of defiance, shouts challenging and threatening.

Assault, a violent attack.

Marshalling, arranging.

Treason, treachery, foul play.

Circuit, a journey around.

Fissure, a split or chasm.

Solemn, awful, serious, grave.

Response, answer, reply.

XVI.—Page 80.

Deeming, believing, thinking.

Onslaught, a fierce attack.

Mannanan Mac Lir, the Pagan Irish sea-god.

XVII.—Page 84.

Billows of war, the tide or onward press of battle.

Wreak, to inflict, to execute.

XVIII.—Page 85.

Incensed, very angry.

Anguish, great grief, pain.

Descendants, children, grand-children, &c.

Spoil, to plunder and pillage.

Illustrious, famous, noble, great.

Marauding, plundering, robbing.

Ravage, to lay waste and plunder.

XIX.—Page 87.

Magic, witchcraft, spells.

Mighty, of wonderful skill.

Distinguish, to tell one from another.

[Pg 216]

Shadowy, uncertain, legendary.

Historic times, when there are true accounts of things that happened.

Professional, following some profession or calling.

Remuneration, payment, salary.

Attached, joined to.

XX.—Page 89.

Reverently, with great respect.

Gaelic, the Irish language.

Lore, learning.

Injunction, an order or charge, an advice that should be followed.

Extract, to take out.

Devotedly, with great and anxious care.

Balm, a sort of ointment that soothes pain and cures.

Sentiments, thoughts, feelings.

Comparatively late, late compared with older times.

Predecessor, one who held an office or place before another.

XXI.—Page 92.

Tradition, accounts handed down from generation to generation.

Provincial, belonging to one of the five provinces of Ireland.

Tests, trials.

Entertaining, amusing, diverting.

Festive, joyous, gay, with feasts.

Sedge, a kind of coarse grass.

Keating: the Rev. Doctor Geoffry Keating, who wrote, in Irish, a well known History of Ireland, full of old stories: died 1644.

Oppression, cruelty, tyranny, hardship.

Suppress, to put down.

Exact, to make people pay.

An Irish poet: Thomas Darcy M'Gee.

Seers: among the Milesians were a good many druids, seers, or prophets.

Strath, the level land along a river at both sides; an *inch*.

Mystic forts, the forts mentioned at page 16: mystic, mysterious.

Cairn-crowned hills, Many hills have cairns on top round which the people often held council meetings.

Elk, very large deer. Elk resorts, places frequented by elks.

Modern, belonging to the present time.

Unconquerably, such that he could not be conquered.

Untarnished, unstained, pure, with out a spot.

XXII.—Page 98.

Plaintive, sad, pitiful.

Hesitation, pause, delay.

Palsy, a sort of sickness that causes shivering or shaking.

Litter, a sort of bed in which a person is carried.

Tumult, great noise and confusion.

XXIII.

Revered, regarded with love, honor, and respect.

Distinguished, eminent, honoured.

Community, a number of persons living together.

Permanent, lasting.

Veneration, love and great respect.

Applicant, a person who applies.

Abbess, the head nun of a convent.

XXIV.—Page 107.

Humility, humbleness, lowliness of mind.

Domestic occupations, the work of the house.

Sward, a grassy place.

Reputation, fame, a great name.

Corresponded with her, wrote letters to her, and received replies.

Chariot, a kind of carriage.

Reproachfully, blaming her severely.

Universe, the whole world.

XXV.—Page 111.

Grave, sober, thoughtful.

Unassuming, modest, not forward.

Talents, great cleverness.

Discipline, strict rules and regulations.

Illustrious, eminent, noble, famous.

Detailed, exact, giving all particulars.

Consolation, comfort, a lightening of trouble.

Magnificent, grand, splendid.

[Pg 217]

Shrine, an ornamental tomb or box: sometimes applied to a small church.

Commemorate, to keep in memory.

Gerald Barry, better known as "Giraldus Cambrensis," *i.e.* Gerald the Welshman (Cambria, one of the old names of Wales).

Fane, a temple, a church.

Long ages of darkness and storm: *i.e.* of wars and troubles.

XXVI.—Page 114.

Scribe, a writer: a person who made it the chief business of his life to copy books.

Expert, skillful, ready.

Accomplished, very skillful.

Devoted, given up to earnestly, attached.

Interlaced, woven in and out.

Magnifying glass, a glass that makes things seen through it seem large.

Composition, a piece of writing, a book.

Library, a collection of books.

Dun, brown.

St. Kieran, or more properly Ciaran, lived in the sixth century.

Clonmacnoise on the Shannon, below Athlone, containing the ruins of what was once a great monastery and college, founded by St. Kieran.

XXVII.—Page 120.

Watch and ward: ward means guard: he stood sentinel.

Scared, frightened.

Humorous, full of humour or fun.

XXVIII.—Page 123.

Stud, a number of horses all kept in one place.

Vicious, wicked, spiteful.

Conan Mail, or Conan the bald: the Fena were always making fun of him, for he was big, fat, gluttonous, a great boast, a great coward, and had an evil tongue.

Unconcernedly, not caring a bit.

Perplexity, difficulty and doubt.

Horrible, hateful.

XXIX.—Page 129.

Took counsel, they advised with one another to know what was best to be done.

Explore, to search.

Dizzy, enough to make one's head giddy.

Pillar-stone, a tall stone standing up, such as we often see in Ireland.

Host, a large body of soldiers.

Decoration, an ornament.

Chase, to ornament with thin coatings of metal on the surface.

Enamelled, ornamented as if with enamel.

XXX.—Page 132.

Wizard champion, a champion having something of the nature of a wizard or enchanter.

Circlet, a long thin plate often worn around the head and forehead.

Determination, a firm resolution to conquer.

Chafe, to vex.

Trophy, a prize taken from an enemy in battle.

Poise, to balance.

Scowl, to frown darkly and wickedly.

Terrify, to frighten.

XXXI.—Page 139.

Advantages, benefits, gains.

Diligent, industrious, hard-working.

Uninhabited, having no people living in it.

Presence, appearance.

Luminous, bright, sparkling.

Enlightenment, knowledge, learning, instruction.

Civilise, to refine, to educate, to bring people to live in a decent and proper way.

Doctrine, teaching, belief, faith.

Structure, a building.

Venerable, old and greatly loved and respected.

Incessant, without ceasing, continual.

Occupation, employment, work.

His relative the king of that part of Scotland: the royal families of Ireland and Scotland were related to each other (see pp. 5and 6), and Columkille was related to both.

[Pg 218]

XXXII.—Page 145.
Voluntary, by his own choice.
Ben Edar, Howth, near Dublin.
Embarking, going on board ship.
Seniors, elderly persons.
Hospice, the part of a monastery set apart for the entertainment of travellers.
Intently, with close attention.

XXXIII.—Page 150.
Heptarchy, means seven kingdoms: for at this time England was divided into seven parts with a king over each.
Relations, connexion, friendship.
Diligence, industry, working steadily.
Intimacy, close friendship.
Foster-son. When a man reared up and educated among his family a boy belonging to another family, he was the foster-father, and the boy was his foster-son.
Bondage, slavery.
Restoration, restoring, giving back.
Marauders, robbers, plunderers.
Intercession, pleading for.
Unfettered of any, not under any other province.
Redundance, more than enough, great plenty.
Historians recording truth: to record truth is the chief merit of a historian.
Bulwark, a safeguard: "Ireland's bulwark," because Tara was in Meath.
Sooth, truth.

XXXIV.—Page 155.
Directions, orders, instructions.
Revellers, persons feasting, drinking, and making merry.
Sack, to plunder and destroy.

XXXV.—Page 158.
Extraordinary, very strange, wonderful.
Keel, the bottom part of a ship or boat.
Astounding, astonishing, wonderful.
Oarstroke of the curragh, about 20 feet.
Circumference, the whole round.
Extending, stretching.
Meshes, the open spaces between the threads of a net.

XXXVI.—Page 162.
Reconcile, to become friends again, to come back to friendship.
Recognise, to know a thing again.
Prow, the head or fore part of a ship or boat.
Affliction, trouble and sorrow.
Reception, receiving or entertaining.
Reveal, to show, to make known.

XXXVII.—Page 164.
Liefer, rather.
Let be this purpose, let it lie by, don't attend to it, don't carry it out: *i.e.* the purpose of revenge.
I let him be, I let him alone.
A tithe, a tenth part.

XXXVIII.—Page 167.
Monastic school, a school kept in a monastery.
Distinguished, eminent and great.

Pilgrimage, a journey to a place for devotion. Pilgrim, a person who goes on a pilgrimage.
Determined will, allowing nothing to turn them from their purpose.
Relinquish, to give up, to abandon.
Luxuries, dainties, delicacies.
Peasantry, the common country people.
Swerve, to turn away from.
Consecrated, made sacred and venerable.
Hermitage, a place where a hermit lives.

XXXIX.—Page 170.
Object of their pilgrimage, the place they chiefly came to visit.
Sojourn, to dwell, to live in a place.
Revere, to regard with honour, love, and respect.
Memorial, something that reminds one of past persons or events.
Vehemently, very earnestly.
Envied, people of other nations envied them, or were jealous of them.
Triumphant, gaining victories.

[Pg 219]

XL.—Page 173.
Successfully cultivated: the Irish people studied and practised them and made improvements.
Pirates, sea robbers.
Permanently, remaining there always.
Expel, to drive out.
Sovereignty, headship, kingship.
Annex, to join.
Encroaching, taking up or advancing on what belongs to another.
Anglo-Irish, partly English and partly Irish.
Milesian stock, the descendants of the Milesians (see p. 2).

XLI.—Page 179.
Croon, a continuous murmuring sort of musical sound or song.
Squire, a gentleman who attended on a knight.
Nier, a river flowing into the Suir from the Co. Waterford.
Spectrally, like a spectre or ghost.
Jack, a leathern jacket used for armour.
Plumes, the feathers of their helmets.

XLII.—Page 181.
Claimant, a person laying claim to something.
Contend, to struggle or fight.
Unimportant, trifling, of no consequence.
Remote, far off, out of the way.
Recognise, to know.
Prostrate, down on hands and knees.
Barons, lords.
Ambush, or ambuscade, an unexpected attack from a hiding place.
Reverses, misfortunes.
Surrender, to give up.
Vigilant, watchful.
Truce, an agreement for peace for a while.
Annals, histories of events as they occurred from year to year.

XLIII.—Page 186.
Cahal-More, Cahal the Great.
Portent, a prodigy, a fearful sign or omen of evil.

Entranced, in a trance, in a vision.
A land of morn, a bright sunny land.
Lustrous, bright, shining with fine crops and flowers.
Resplendent, splendid, sunny, bright.
Anon, immediately, on the spot.
Port sublime, stately and grand looking.
Him queried I, I asked him.
Golden time, a prosperous plentiful time.
Bland, soft, mild, temperate.
Dome, a grand building.
As by a spell, as if by magic; it started up suddenly.
Remember this is all in a dream.
Lyres, harps.
Wreathèd swell, sounding all together with sweet musical turns and shakes.
Thrilling, moving the feelings and heart.
Aghast, frightened, pale with fear.
Minstrel group, those who had been playing the harps.
'Twas then the time we were in the days. The poet means:—"Something dreadful has clearly happened; but how can this be, since this is the reign of Cahal-More?" He did not know—in his dream—of Cahal's death.
Fleckt, spotted.
Alien sun, a strange sun: it was of course strange, for it glared from the *north*.
Shorn beams, not bright, giving a dull gloomy sort of light.
Skeleton: the skeleton of a man, a sign of disaster: the skeleton, and the blood spots in the sky, and the "alien sun" were some of the portents.
Castled Maine: there are many castles along its banks.
Teuton, a German.
XLIV.—Page 190.
Expedition, an undertaking or journey.
Onslaught, a violent attack.
Tunic, a loose outer garment.
Dominions, territories.
[Pg 220]
XLV.—Page 193.
Disdain, to scorn, to hate.
Commendations, praises.
Do homage, to yield obedience.
Apprehend, to take prisoner.
Devise, to plan.
Confer, to take counsel.
Battle-harness, battle dress with arms.
Apparel, clothes.
Passport, permission in writing to pass from one country to another.
Subscribe, to write one's name.
Servitor, one in the king's service.
Furniture: *i.e.* the furniture of a ship—oars, sails, cordage, &c.
Ensample, old form of *example*.
XLVI.—Page 197.
Evil plight, miserable state.
Council, a number of men kept by the king to help him with their advice.
Enterprise, an undertaking.
Perilous, dangerous.
Peer, an equal, a match.
Stalworth, strong, stout, brave.

Knightly, like a knight, valiant and stout-hearted.
Seemly, proper, decent.
XLVII.—Page 200.
Lists, the enclosed ground where a single combat was to be fought.
Obeisance, courtesy, saluting, bowing to.
Banquet, a feast.
Reverence, great respect.
Deeming, believing, thinking. [Entry copied from XVI.—Page 80.
Intently, with attention, closely.
Grim, very fierce and angry.
XLVIII.—Page 203.
Baron, a lord of the lowest rank. The ranks are:—baron, viscount, earl, marquis, duke.
Independent, not under the authority of anyone.
Goodly presence, a noble or fine appearance.
Appease, to pacify.
Hobby, a middle-sized horse of Irish breed, much valued.
Adversary, an opponent, an enemy.
Discord, disagreement, quarrelling.
Jars, wrangles, quarrels.
Chapter house, a house or room in a cathedral where the clergy meet.
Trice, a very short time, as long as one would take to count three.
Outface, to dare him up to his face.
Green wound, a fresh wound.
Devise, to plan.
Bungerlie, in a bungling manner.
XLIX.—Page 208.
Cultivate, to study, practise, and improve.
Colonists, persons who leave their native land and settle in some distant country.
Dirge, a mournful or funeral song.
Dialogue, two people speaking in turn, conversation between two.
Interrupt, to stop for a time.
Placid, quiet, gentle, peaceful.
Resume, to take up again.
Clansmen, the men belonging to a clan.
National music, music that has grown up gradually among the people of a country.
Originally, in the beginning.

FOOTNOTES:
[1] It is necessary to know the substance of this first sketch in order to understand the rest of the book.
[2] Inisfail, one of the old names of Ireland.
[3] Miled, pronounced *Mee-lĕ* (two syllables).
[4] The Anglo-Norman Invasion will be found described at page 175.
[5] Demons of the air were evil spirits who were supposed to live, not in underground places like fairies, but in the air. They were very much dreaded and hated.
[6] Among the ancient Irish Romantic Tales, three are specially known as "The Three Sorrowful Stories of Erin," viz. "The Fate of the Children of Lir," "The Fate of the Sons of Turenn," both of which relate to the Dedannans; and "The Fate of the Sons of Usna," referring to the Milesian people. The greater part of the

"Children of Lir" and the whole of the "Sons of Usna" are given in this book, translated from the Gaelic. "The Fate of the Sons of Turenn" is translated in full in "Old Celtic Romances."

[7] Lake Darvra, now Lough Derravaragh, in Westmeath.

[8] The sea between Erin and Alban (Ireland and Scotland) was anciently called the Sea of Moyle, from the Moyle, or Mull, of Cantire.

[9] Inish Glora; a small island, about five miles west from Belmullet, in the county Mayo, still known by the same name.

[10] The Taillkenn, a name given by the druids to St. Patrick.

[11] Three hundred years: the Dedannans were regarded as gods and lived an immensely long time.

[12] Carricknarone, the "Rock of the Seals": probably the Skerry rock near Portrush in Antrim: but the old name is now forgotten.

[13] Short Irish poems often began and ended in the same words, as seen in the above translation.

[14] In Ireland, in old times, the dead were often buried standing up in the grave. It was in this way Finola and her brothers were buried.

[15] Ogham, a sort of writing often used on tombstones to mark the names of the persons buried. It consisted of lines and points generally cut on the edges of the stone.

[16] Clonard, in Meath, on the Boyne. Bangor, in the Co. Down.

[17] St. Augustine came to England in the year 596—having been sent by Pope Gregory—and converted to Christianity those of the English who had not been already converted.

[18] Quelna or Cooley, the ancient name of the hilly peninsula lying between the bays of Carlingford and Dundalk: the name Cooley is still retained.

[19] The translation that follows is quite new, and is now published for the first time. On this fine story is founded the poem of "Deirdre" by Robert Dwyer Joyce, M.D.

[20] Ulaid (pron. *Ulla*), Ulster.

[21] The druids professed to be able to foretell by observing the stars and clouds.

[22] "Deirdre" is said to mean "alarm."

[23] That is 1665. This inverted method of enumeration was often used in Ireland. But they also used direct enumeration like ours.

[24] This and the other places named in Deirdre's Farewell are all in the west of Scotland.

[25] Irish name *Drum-Sailech*; the ridge on which Armagh was afterwards built.

[26] These champions, as well as their wives, took care never to show any signs of fear or alarm even in the time of greatest danger: so Naisi and Deirdre kept playing quietly as if nothing was going on outside, though they heard the din of battle resounding.

[27] The "Three *Tonns* or Waves of Erin" were the Wave of Tuath outside the mouth of the river Bann, off the coast of Derry; the Wave of Rury in Dundrum Bay, off the county Down; and the Wave of Cleena in Glandore Harbour in the south of Cork. In stormy weather, when the wind blows from certain directions, the sea at those places, as it tumbles over the sandbanks, or among the caves and fissures of the rocks, utters a loud and solemn roar, which in old times was believed to forebode the death of some king.

The legends also tell that the shield belonging to a king moaned when the person who wore it in battle—whether the king himself or a member of his family—was in danger of death: the moan was heard all over Ireland; and the "Three Waves of Erin" roared inresponse. See "Irish Names of Places," Vol. II., Chap. XVI.

[28] Slieve Cullinn, now Slieve Gullion mountain in Armagh.

[29] The Red Branch Knights were all pagans; and besides, what they meant here by revenge was merely punishment for a great crime.

[30] The Brehon Law: that is, the old law of Ireland.

[31] Van Helmont.

[32] Fena, spelled *Fianna* in Irish, and pronounced *Feena*.

[33] The above account of how the Fena hunted, cooked, ate, and slept is from Keating, who took it from old Irish books.

[34] "The Pursuit of the Gilla Dacker and his horse" is a humorousstory, of which only a few incidents are given here. The Gilla Dacker was really Mannanan Mac Lir, the Pagan Irish sea-god, who came in disguise to play a trick—a sort of practical joke—on the Fena. The whole story is given in "Old Celtic Romances."

[35] Knockainey: a hill celebrated in story, rising over the village of Knockainey, in the Co. Limerick.

[36] Fomor, a gigantic warrior, a giant: its real meaning is "a sea-robber," commonly called a Fomorian.

[37] Gilla Dacker means "a slothful fellow"—a fellow hard to move, hard to manage, hard to have anything to do with.

[38] The ancient Irish used drinking vessels of various forms and with several names. A "Drinking-horn" (called a *corn*: pronounced*curn*) was usually made of a bullock's horn, hollowed out, cut into shape, and often highly ornamented with silver rim, precious stones, carvings, and other decorations. A beautiful drinking-horn will be found figured in the "Child's History of Ireland," p. 26. Another kind of drinking vessel—the mether—has been already noticed here (page 17 above).

[39] In books he is often called Columba; but in Ireland he is best known by the name Columkille. This is derived from *colum* [pron.*collum*] a dove, and *cill*, or *kill*, a church: the "Dove of the church." This name was given him when a boy from his gentle, affectionate disposition, and because he was so fond of praying in the little church of Tullydouglas, near where he was born: so that the little boys who were accustomed to play with him used often to ask: "Has our little *Colum* yet come from the church?"

The sketch given here is taken chiefly, but not altogether, from Adamnan's "Life of St. Columba." Adamnan was a native of Tirconnell or Donegal, like Columba himself. He died in the year 703. He was the ninth abbot of Iona, of which Columba was the first. His "Life of St. Columba" is a very beautiful piece of Latin composition.

[40] Glastonbury, a town in Somersetshire, in England, where in old times there was a celebrated monastery, much reported to by Irish students.

[41] This simple and beautiful narrative of the last days of St. Columkille, including the two pleasing little stories about the crane and the old white horse, with the affecting account of the saint's death, is taken altogether from Adamnan's Life. The circumstances of Columkille's death are, in some respects, very like those attending the death of the Venerable Bede, as recorded in the tender and loving letter of his pupil, the monk Cuthbert. But Adamnan's narrative was written more than forty years before that of Cuthbert.
Baithen was St. Columkille's first cousin and his most beloved disciple, and succeeded him as abbot of Iona.

[42] This Alfred must be distinguished from Alfred the Great who lived two centuries later.

[43] Meath, one of the five Kingdoms into which Ireland was divided. Ben-Edar, the old name of Howth, near Dublin.

[44] It was translated very exactly into prose in 1832 by the great Irish scholar Dr. John O'Donovan: the Irish poet James Clarence Mangan turned this prose with very little change into verse, part of which is given here.

[45] Cruachan or Croghan in the north of the present Co. Roscommon, the ancient palace of the kings of Connaught: see page 52.

[46] Slewmargy, now Slievemargy, a low range of hills in Queen's County.

[47] Only a few of his adventures are given here: but the whole story of the voyage is in "Old Celtic Romances": see page 164, farther on.

[48] Thomond, North Munster, namely the present county Clare and parts of Tipperary and Limerick.

[49] Curragh, a boat made of basket or wicker work, covered with hides. Curraghs were generally small and light: but some, intended for long voyages, were large and strong, and covered with two, or three, layers of hide one outside another. Sometimes the hides were tanned into leather to give additional strength.

[50] For the Book of the Dun Cow and the Yellow Book of Lecan, see p. 118.

[51] St. Brendan of Clonfert in Kerry, commonly called Brendan the Navigator: born in Kerry in 484. He sailed from near Brandon mountain in Kerry (which is named from him) on his celebrated voyage of seven years on the Atlantic, in which it is related he saw many wonderful things—quite as wonderful as those of Maildune.

[52] The Isle of Finn: i.e. of Finn Mac Cumaill: Ireland (see p. 92).

[53] Fiesole in Tuscany, Italy: pronounced in four syllables: Fee-ess'-o-lĕ.

[54] In the "Child's History of Ireland" there is a picture of the round tower and church ruins on this little island.

[55] I.e. enrolled in books under the name of Scotia. The natives always called it Erin.

[56] Ireland had mines of gold in old times; and silver was also found. Great numbers of Irish gold ornaments, found from time to time in the earth, are now preserved in Museums.

[57] Pearls were then found in many Irish rivers; as they are, sometimes, to this day.

[58] The Venerable Bede, a great English historian, writing in the eighth century, calls Ireland "a land flowing with milk and honey."

[59] Ireland was noted for the plenty and goodness of its wool.

[60] Ireland had great warriors, and many learned men and skilful artists (see pp. 20, 47, and 117).

[61] There are no venomous reptiles in Ireland. There were then no frogs: but these were afterwards introduced from England.

[62] Cong in Mayo, between Lough Corrib and Lough Mask; the remains of an abbey are there still.

[63] Knockmoy in Galway, six miles from Tuam: the ruins of the abbey still remain.

[64] Mangan wrote many poetical translations from the Irish, as well as from the German and other languages. The "Vision of Connaught" is, however, an original poem, not a translation.

[65] Irish, Ceann [can], meaning 'head,' one of the Gaelic titles for a chief.

[66] Prince Arthur, the rightful heir to the English throne, was cast into prison by John: he was soon after murdered, which, it was believed, was done by John's orders.

[67] At this time the kings of England had a large territory in France so that quarrels often arose between them and the French kings.

[68] A further account of the Great Earl, and of some of his proceedings, will be found in the "Child's History of Ireland."

Made in the USA
Las Vegas, NV
14 December 2024

14232169R00079